Cutting Costs in the Medical Practice

Second Edition

Alan S. Whiteman, PhD, FACMPE

Jerry Hermanson, MBA, CHE

Dennis Palkon, PhD, MPH, MSW

**GREENBRANCH
PUBLISHING**

Phoenix, Maryland

Cutting Costs in the Medical Practice

Second Edition

Copyright © 2006 by Greenbranch Publishing, LLC
ISBN: 0-9768343-0-8

Published by Greenbranch Publishing, LLC
PO Box 208
Phoenix, MD 21131
Phone: (800) 933-3711
Fax: (410) 329-1510
Email: info@greenbranch.com
Website: www.mpmnetwork.com, www.soundpractice.net

Requests for permission, information on our multi-copy pricing program, or other information should be addressed to the Permissions Department, Greenbranch Publishing, LLC.

This publication is designed to provide general medical practice management information and is sold with the understanding that neither the author nor the publisher is engaged in rendering legal, accounting, ethical, or clinical advice. If legal or other expert advice is required, the services of a competent professional person should be sought.

Printed in the United States of America by United Book Press, Inc. www.unitedbookpress.com

Publisher
Nancy Collins

Editorial Assistant
Jennifer Weiss

Book Designer
Laura Carter
Carter Publishing Studio

Index
Deborah K. Tourtlotte

Contents

Preface

Medical practices operate in a dynamic environment that is constantly changing. Due to managed care and constant legislative changes, physicians face increasing demand for clinical services, placing more and more demand on office staff. In order to manage their practice effectively, physicians must gain significant knowledge in a variety of areas in which they may not have professional training, such as accounting, financial management, purchasing, and human resource management.

The intent of this second edition is to further explain the basic steps that may be followed by a medical practice to reduce operating overhead and enhance productivity for the physician(s) and office staff. In addition, this second edition provides updated information and resources for continuously enhanced electronic systems. Through practical information that may be directly applied to practice operations, this book is designed to be used as a tool to assist physicians in making decisions as they relate to the daily and long-term operations of the medical practice.

Some of the most important decisions a physician makes have long-term implications. Therefore, it is critical that the physician has a strong knowledge base when making major purchases or drastically altering the way a medical practice operates. For example, the physician's position can be strongly enhanced in negotiations by knowing the right questions to ask and being able to properly evaluate the answers received.

The ever-changing healthcare environment also dictates that a physician be able to operate a medical practice like a business. This business must effectively utilize scarce resources and provide quality medical care and outstanding patient service. Only with an understanding of the information provided in this book can a physician begin to develop an information base to make informed and intelligent decisions.

Acknowledgments

The authors would like to thank Lisa Fisher, MHA for her efforts in reviewing the text and offering timely suggestions for updates. We, also, appreciate the efforts of Monica Lee for assisting us with formatting and editorial issues.

About the Authors

Alan S. Whiteman, Ph.D., FACMPE, is an Associate Dean for Health Sciences and graduate professor of graduate health administration studies at Barry University, Miami Shores, Florida. Dr. Whiteman is, also, an experienced healthcare executive with over 35 years' experience in all facets of the healthcare industry with over 24 years' experience in managing or consulting with physicians practices of all sizes and structures. In addition, he is a principal of Healthcare Integration Consultants, Inc., a professional services firm specializing in assisting physicians in making practices more efficient, effective and financially sound. He received his Ph.D. from Walden University, his MBA from Wayne State University and his BA from Michigan State University.

Jerry Hermanson, MBA, CHE, is an experienced health care leader. Mr Hermanson has over 27 years' experience in the industry, including hospital administration, physician organizations, and managed care. Mr Hermanson is chief executive officer of Healthcare Integration Consultants, Inc. In this capacity he provides management and technical services to IPAs, physician practices of all sizes, and medical societies. He is also an adjunct professor of graduate health administration studies. He received his MBA and BSBA from the University of Florida.

Dennis Palkon, PhD, MPH, MSW, is a full professor and past chairman of Health Administration at Florida Atlantic University in Boca Raton, Florida. Dr Palkon has extensive academic and publishing experience. He is also executive editor of *Hospital Topics* and serves on numerous editorial boards. He received his PhD and MPH from the University of Pittsburgh, his MSW from Virginia Commonwealth, and his BS from Villanova University.

Chapter 1

Identifying Areas of Concern

Employing systematic methods to identify a medical practice's expenses and whether the expenses are reasonable is a basic requirement when attempting to contain costs. In addition, an ongoing review of expenses is necessary to ensure continued efforts in cost containment.

There are a number of management tools you can develop to assist you in making such expense determinations. In general, these tools collect data and give you the ability to compare the expenses of your own practice over time or to compare expenses against other practices. Most of these tools are simple in concept and implementation. However, the key to the success of these tools is your ability to accurately identify costs in your practice. If your practice is large, it may already have an accounting system in place that captures the expense data on a regular basis. Such a system can divide practice expenses into categories and can generate regular reports. Smaller groups or solo practices may not have the same accounting capabilities. In these practices it is necessary to work with whoever is providing bookkeeping services and develop a regular method to identify the practices' expenses and separate them into expense categories.

Once an accurate system to identify expenses is in place, you can begin to develop tools to search for cost savings. Areas of concern are usually identified by comparing your practice's costs against internal expectations and external data. It is important to perform both internal and external comparisons to maximize your efforts at cost containment.

Reports of practice expenses must be produced on a monthly basis to be helpful in identifying areas of potential cost savings.

Internal Comparisons

Comparing your actual costs with expected costs requires the development of internal target costs or expenses. This process is known as *budgeting* and is a basic management activity for any size practice.

According to David H. Glusman, CPA, an expense budget is the simplest tool to maintain control over expenses.[1] An expense budget provides a template to identify what you think your expenses should be versus your actual expenses. A difference between your actual expenses and what you budgeted indicates a possible area of cost concern.

Budget Development

Some look at the process of developing a budget as difficult and laborious. But, shared with the key individuals in a practice—including key physicians and managers—the task can be accomplished in a relatively short period of time and may give all participants a new view of how the practice is spending its money.

In developing an expense budget you must first make a list of the various expenses incurred by your practice. This list should include all areas of expenditure except physicians' compensation. In making a list you should refer to your practice's "chart of accounts," which may have been developed by your practice manager or your accountant. This chart of accounts should list all of the expense categories that your accounting system is capturing. It should include areas of general overhead such as rent, telephone expense, utilities, waste removal, and so on. In addition, it should identify various types of supplies used in the practice such as general office supplies, medical supplies, laboratory supplies (if your practice has an in-house lab), or other categories of supplies unique to your practice. This list should also include expenses related to your employees such as salaries, benefit costs, payroll taxes, and other employee-related expenses.

When this list of expense categories has been compiled, the next step is to estimate projected expenditures for each. A good way to begin the process of projecting future expenditures is to compile data organized by expense category from the last several years. By analyzing how your costs have changed over time, you can establish trends that can be the basis of future projections.

Some expense categories will trend based on preestablished formulas and can therefore be estimated with a high degree of accuracy. Expenses such as rent, leases, and other contracted services fall into this type. A review of contracts will give you the basis to establish future cost projections in these expense categories.

Other expenses will trend based on business factors, such as inflation or cost of production. Expenses in this category include most supplies, utility costs, insurance costs, and staff salaries. A percentage increase to these expenses can be established by reviewing projected increases in the consumer price index for medical services and by asking the practice's suppliers if they have projections for future price increases.

In addition, most expenses are affected by the volume of care given in the practice. To factor this in, a percentage increase in service volume must be projected and then applied to those expense categories affected by volume increases before other factors are considered (such as inflation). While some categories of expenses will vary consistently and uniformly with the increase in volume (such as medical supplies, office supplies, and lab supplies), others will occur in steps (such as salaries and equipment costs). Accurately predicting these categories of expenses will be the most difficult.

Budget Comparison

Usually an annual budget that is broken down into monthly projections is developed, as it may be easier to project what the practice's expenditures are on a monthly basis and then compile an annual figure. Whichever method is used, it is important to try and identify how these expenses will fluctuate from month to month. Some expenses will be consistent from month to month, such as rent, while others will change based on volatile factors, such as volume of care given (ie, supplies). Still others will vary based on payment schedules, such as employee taxes and other insurance expenses. A review of historic expenditures will give a good indication of which categories will change from month to month and which will be consistent.

Once an expense budget is finalized it can become a powerful tool to identify where the practice is incurring its costs. To effectively utilize an expense budget, however, actual expenditures must be reviewed on at least a monthly basis. Variations between actual and projected spending should be carefully researched to determine the cause of the variation and whether there is need to make any changes affecting the expenditures.

While the practice manager should make the initial review of the monthly expense report and research explanations for any variances discovered, the practice's managing physician must do the final review. If effective cost containment is to be accomplished, the physician must take a leadership role and be directly involved in the budgeting process on a regular basis. Such involvement does not have to be time-consuming, but it must be consistent. Review of the expense budget performance can be made a regular part of your monthly management meeting with your key office staff and physician group, for example.

Payroll Reports

While salary expenses are part of your overall expense budget, you will need to develop an additional report to properly review these expenses. A *payroll report* comparing actual hours worked to budgeted hours helps to identify excessive costs.

Practices that have part-time employees must have a report that compares actual hours worked with budgeted hours. A simple look at overtime will not readily identify excess hours worked by part-time employees, as excess hours will not generate overtime situations unless the employee works more than 40 hours during a given week. Therefore, a report listing each employee's scheduled hours and actual hours worked should be generated for each pay period. This report can be reviewed monthly with the general expense budget comparisons.

When looking at a payroll report, it is important to look at regular hours worked as well as overtime hours.

Included in the payroll report should be a list, by employee, of all overtime paid. As overtime is usually paid on a time-and-a-half basis, a reduction or elimination of any overtime is key for cost containment. If you are routinely scheduling overtime because the practice's patient volume is growing, careful, ongoing analysis should be undertaken to determine when it is financially beneficial to hire new employees who can be paid for regular hours.

Most formal in-house payroll systems and all outside payroll service companies can provide payroll reports on a routine basis. Again, review them at
least monthly.

External Comparisons

Comparing your practice's expenses or performance to outside indicators is
another source of identifying areas of potential cost containment. This process
is sometimes referred to as *benchmarking*. According to Joan M. Roediger, JD,
LLM, benchmarking provides a more structured approach to establishing business parameters and reviewing financial progress against baseline values.[2]

Physician practices can take advantage of these techniques by obtaining
benchmark data from outside sources and comparing the data against their
performance. Most outside benchmarks are based on surveys of other medical
practices in the same geographic area as your practice as well as nationwide.

Sources of Benchmark Data

There are numerous organizations that collect data that can be used for
comparison against your practice. These sources include the American
Medical Association, numerous health care magazines, professional and specialty societies for both physicians and health care consultants, and various
local organizations. In addition, a careful review of medical publications
can yield a wealth of sources from surveys that are available for the asking.

Many of these sources look at a very limited set of data. Others, such as
the Medical Group Management Association's (MGMA) annual survey of
physician group practices, provide data for numerous expense and revenue
categories based on geographic region, medical specialty, group size, and
several other parameters.

It is also possible to develop local or regional data through surveys you and
your colleagues may agree to develop and compile. This can be particularly
helpful if your area is unique due to local factors. For example, data such as
salary costs can vary greatly over larger geographic areas, so local surveys
may be the best source of good comparative data. Consider asking your
county medical society to help develop benchmark data.

Validation of Benchmark Data

Before you compare benchmark data against your practice, you must understand the method used to solicit the data as well as the definitions used in the surveys. The data gathered may not be directly comparable to your practice's data, or you may need to recalculate your practice's data in order to compare it against the benchmark data. Data that are given for large geographic areas may not be meaningful for your particular area, for example. Rural and urban data, likewise, may not be comparable.

Data that are collected for specific specialty practices is generally better for comparison. However, try to determine what services or procedures are included in the practices surveyed, as that may have a significant effect on the comparability of the data to your practice.

Benchmark Data on Practice Expenses

For purposes of cost containment, only benchmark data on expenses are relevant. You may, however, wish to look at other types of data with which to compare your practice, such as revenue and productivity data. Revenue and compensation data are always important to physicians and are natural categories to review at least on a yearly basis. These comparisons are particularly important when considering the addition of a new physician or physician extender to a practice. (See Chapter 6 for information on recruiting additional practitioners.)

Overhead generally runs between 55% and 65% of total revenue.[3] This excludes compensation paid to physicians. As a result, significant savings can result in higher compensation to physicians. Therefore, a comparison of your practice's overhead to national and regional data for your specialty is a key expenses factor to benchmark.

Data on the various components of the practice's overhead can also be compared. The number of personnel per physician is another key comparison, as salary costs can run as high as 50% of the overhead of a practice. In addition, salaries for each category of employee are an important item to compare—in tight labor markets, low salaries can make it difficult to attract and retain good employees.

Other data categories include virtually all other expense categories for which you can receive data. The more you compare, the better a picture you get of your practice in relation to others.

Analysis of External Data

External data that represent overall practice performance, such as total overhead as a percent of revenue, should be compared on an annual basis. Monthly data or other periods of less than a year may be affected by seasonal fluctuations in your practice's expenses. Even individual expense category data are not comparable over short periods.

Data that identify categories that do not change much with time can be compared on a one-shot basis. Salary levels are an example of data that are comparable with your current figures. Other examples include annual malpractice premiums, other annual insurance premiums, and individual supply items.

Guidelines for Comparing Data

Once the comparative data have been validated to your satisfaction, variations from your performance against the benchmark data will begin to be of value. However, it is important to fully research any significant differences between your practice's data and the internal or external data.

Unique factors within your practice must be considered before a final determination is made as to whether your costs are reasonable. Often, budget comparisons, particularly in the first year or two, will show variations due to inaccurate budgeting. Your budgeting accuracy will improve with time.

Carefully validate the data you are using and make comparisons of similar expense categories for the most accurate time period. Developing a handful of reports that you regularly review will give you the tools needed to identify potential cost savings for your practice. It can also give you better knowledge with which you can oversee your practice.

External data usually represent general averages or ranges of expenses collected by a single or specific survey. Averages may not be good indicators if the response to the survey was low. A good survey will indicate the percentage of responses or give other data that will help you decide if the figures are worth using. In addition, external data that are developed from multiple specialty practices may not yield comparable data for your specialty.

Endnotes

1. Glusman DII. Benchmarking physician practice expenses. *Physician's News Digest.* May 1999.

2. Roediger JM. Formally benchmarking your medical practice. *Physician's News Digest.* August 1999.

3. Kostreski F, ed. Managing your practice to lower overhead. *Pediatric News.* 1997.

Chapter 2

Work Smarter, Not Harder! A Systems Approach

*D*r Brown entered his office at 9:15 AM after completing two complex hospital visits. The lobby was filled with patients and the staff was scrambling to deal with the morning's myriad of problems. Because of the health care industry changes that had occurred in recent years, such as the increase in managed care and numerous regulatory requirements placed on practices, the staff continuously "plugged holes in the dike" to get the various required tasks completed and have the patients see Dr Brown. Unfortunately, because of increased workloads, high turnover, and confusing and cumbersome rules and regulations, the practice was in chaos and the staff demoralized.

Many physician practices have experienced an increase in both patient and paperwork loads, an increase in demand for physician and staff time, and a reduction in revenue. These factors have been greatly exaggerated by the fact that many medical offices evolved without formal planning or design. Thus, when more demands are made on an already taxed system, the system collapses.

If Dr Brown's scenario sounds familiar, it is time to look at the potential benefits of re-engineering and process improvement. *Re-engineering* is the task of reviewing the practice operation and finding a simpler and more efficient method to complete all of the tasks involved in operating the practice. *Process improvement* entails reviewing each procedure and methodology that is used and finding a more effective and less labor-intensive way to complete that task.

In today's office environment, the mention of re-engineering often causes an immediate reaction to begin automating all office functions. While automation is an option, focusing strictly on automation becomes too narrow a scope. (Examples of automated systems include patient scheduling and accounts receivable management. Manual systems might include such functions as patient flow in the practice or telephone communications.)

There is a definite need for a combination of automated and manual systems that interface to fulfill the needs of the medical practice. This chapter discusses how to review your practice, how to review both types of systems at work in your practice, and how, if properly designed and utilized, these systems can reduce physician downtime and reduce staff stress.

Reviewing Your Practice

The only means to improve your practice's operations is to review and revise the systems that are currently in place. Thus, the first step in reviewing, or re-engineering, your practice is to thoroughly examine and record each step that is taken in the completion of various tasks.

The most effective way to record a procedure is to either write a brief step-by-step summary or sketch out the workflow in a diagram. It is extremely important for the individual reviewing the work process to understand the nuances of the specific tasks being studied. Make sure that you repeatedly ask the individual who performs each task to go over each step and to not leave out any details. Once the procedures are documented, observe the individuals performing the tasks on several occasions to ensure that you have not missed a key step in your documentation.

A key question to ask your employees or your office manager is how a specific procedure evolved. This question should be followed by further questions, asking why this procedure is followed and how long it has been performed in this manner.

Manual Systems

The financial success of a medical practice is completely dependent on physician productivity, which is driven by efficiently and effectively seeing patients and performing procedures day after day. By optimizing physician productivity, the practice also increases patient satisfaction and enhances referral opportunities. Thus, the strategic areas in your practice that will benefit the most from re-engineering and process improvement pertain to patient-related processes. These include the following manual systems: telephone communications, patient scheduling, and practice flow.

The best place to start an assessment of practice systems is at the practice's initial point of contact with a patient: the telephone call received from a patient. This initial contact with the patient, the information exchanged, and processing the information are the first steps in a manual process that have a critical impact on the practice operations and the cost of operating the practice. Effective and efficient systems reduce operating overhead and constantly play a key role in containing costs, which ultimately can lead to increased revenues.

Keep Staff Involved

It is important to remember that the most complex part of making changes in a business entity, particularly in a medical practice, is gaining the full support and cooperation of your staff. Employees who do not understand the sudden desire to change "the way things have always been done" may resist the change and can defeat the re-engineering process. Therefore, it is imperative that, prior to beginning the re-engineering process, you communicate your goals and objectives to your staff, solicit their support, and explain the direct benefits to them. Remember, consistent two-way communication with your employees is the key to your success!

Telephone Communications   During an initial review of the telephone system, it is important to separate the electronic communication system from the manual aspects of human intervention. The key to successful evaluation of the telephone communication system is to evaluate the following:

1. **Greeting of the caller.** The staff person answering the telephone should establish the caller's identity.

2. **Triage of the call.** Is the call a medical issue? Billing issue? If the caller is a patient, does he or she want to make an appointment? Need directions? Or is it a nonmedical call?

3. **Length of initial call.** Does the staff person greet the caller, triage the call, and satisfy the caller's needs in a reasonable amount of time?

Experienced employees should be able to effectively greet a caller, triage the call, and meet the caller's initial needs in less than one minute. If calls are taking longer on a regular basis, then the employee is not judiciously managing his or her time. Employees answering the telephones should have a standardized script that they use on all calls. This script can be modified to adapt to callers they know or to deal with unusual circumstances.

Managing the telephone process properly will alleviate one of the biggest bottlenecks in patient flow that occurs in a medical office. Automated telephone attendants and other electronic systems can enhance and improve a good manual system, but they are only a stopgap measure if a good flow and system are not in place.

Once a good system is designed and implemented telephone software enhancements can reduce staff workloads and expedite practice efficiencies. Consideration should give telephone software that directs callers through specific prompts to leave prescription refill requests, nursing calls, calls for physicians, directions to the practice and a myriad of other options.

Upon completion of the review of the telephone answering process, it is important to review each problem or bottleneck, prepare a solution for the problem, and teach the employees the proper method of handling each situation. Role-playing, if properly utilized, is a tool that can be used at a staff meeting to teach proper telephone technique. A sound telephone response system can also reduce stress and the need to hire additional personnel.

Increased patient flow does not mean less patient service.[1] Therefore, during the scheduling review process, throw out preconceived concepts and look for new ways to enhance the process.

Patient Scheduling   Once the telephone communications system has been reviewed and the office staff trained on the proper use of the system, scheduling patient visits is the next critical area to review. A good scheduling system can increase physician productivity, increase practice revenue, and help contain labor costs.

Stop thinking in blocks of 10, 15, 20, and 30 minutes. Instead, look at the system as scheduling for the specific problem. Some patients may only need a few minutes with the doctor, for example, and most visits could be categorized into *short, medium,* or *long.*[2]

The key element to scheduling goes back to the quality of the initial telephone communication: finding out what the patient needs when the appointment is scheduled. Experience with the practice will enable you to determine how many visits of each category appear in the practice each day.

Once the current patient scheduling system has been reviewed and revisions are proposed, prepare a written procedure that explains in detail the process to be followed. To ensure that the procedure will work, review the proposed process with your staff, get their input, and fine-tune the procedure. After the procedure is implemented, periodically review the process and make sure it is being followed. Changing behavior is a difficult and complex process. If the changes are not monitored continuously, individuals may revert to old behavior.

Upon the successful implementation of new scheduling procedures, the practice can begin the process of using an electronic scheduling system. Remember, automation is not a substitute for good procedures—it is just a means of enhancing and streamlining a good work process.

Practice Flow   One of the basics of efficient and effective office operation is the patient and staff traffic flow as they move through the office all day long. This traffic flow has significant ramifications on the entire practice. The traffic pattern in the practice determines the number of staff members with patient contact and the number of employees required to process the patients. If you reduce the number of staff necessary for regular face-to-face patient contact, you can reduce the office traffic and possibly the number of employees.[3]

Many practices have employees literally tripping over each other and the patients. Why? Because no one has defined their job responsibilities or provided a defined workstation for their duties. It is important that employees have job descriptions that explain their roles and responsibilities.

It is also critical that, as the practice is being reviewed, the patient flow is tracked for a period of time to learn exactly how and why a patient is managed in a specific way. One must define all of the steps to determine if parts of the process are unnecessary, are duplicated by the physician, or have simply "always been done this way." Remember, if the patient is not in the room waiting for the doctor, the practice has just increased inefficiency and decreased physician productivity.

During the review process, carefully observe the check-in and check-out areas of the practice. It is important to make sure that there is enough space during peak periods to handle the volume of patients requiring assistance. During this observation, make sure that your staffing patterns enable adequate staff to support each function during peak periods.

Today, electronic media can be used supplement the practice's staff through the use of practice websites and in office computers. If the practice has a website, patients who are comfortable using computers could be instructed to go to the website and complete registration forms. In addition, computers could be placed in the lobby for patients to fill out registration forms, eliminating a duplication of effort by the staff and alleviating the need to interpret bad hand writing. Carrying this one step further, offices with modern practice management systems can scan insurance cards and other demographic information into the system without making copies and typing forms.

While eliminating delays in the traffic flow process is essential, it is important to provide the patients with a pleasant lobby while waiting to be seen. Attention must be paid to keeping new magazines in the lobby, playing music and/or providing televisions for patient viewing. Electronic devices provide the practice with a means of marketing new services, providing patient education and encouraging good health habits.

In many cases, the physician is a key contributor to traffic interruptions in the practice. Most doctors have good work habits and stay focused on patient care during office hours. But, in some instances, the staff, through poor communication about office procedures, disrupts the traffic flow by taking the doctor out of production. It is imperative that once the doctor begins seeing patients he or she is not interrupted (except for urgent patient care issues or for specific reasons the doctor has communicated to the staff).

Office Layout   In the process of reviewing manual systems in the practice, it is important to also look at the physical layout of the practice site. The practice site was, most likely, established at the onset of your practice, and in many cases, the practice has evolved into something different. Undoubtedly, the volume of patients has increased significantly. Unless the review determines that the practice site is too small or will not meet future practice demands, the most expedient activity is to enhance the practice through the review and modification process.

Patient Education   Reviewing the manual systems and implementing effective procedures is only half of the battle. The other half of the battle is educating patients on office policy and procedure. This is a crucial step if practice economies and effectiveness are to be accomplished.

Educating patients is accomplished through a combination of methods. First, the practice should instruct the patient on office policy each time he or she calls the office. Staff may tell the patient that he or she must arrive 15 minutes early to complete paperwork or that he or she must bring a specimen, and so on. This must be reinforced at the visit by the staff reminding the patients of their responsibilities. In addition, the office should provide written literature in the lobby and in the exam rooms regarding the procedures the patients must follow.

Electronic Systems

Once the practice has completed its fine-tuning of the manual systems it uses throughout its daily operation, it is time to focus on the practice's automated systems.

Cost Containment

Our goal is to contain cost and reduce overhead—not to look for increasing expenses.

During the entire review process our energies have been focused on stream-lining the office and improving the practice's manual systems. The key benefit of this process is to maximize the utilization of office personnel. Human resources are the most costly element in your practice. Thus, it is critical that you use this resource effectively and conserve it. If the practice is properly reviewed and modified, problems will be solved and additional staff will not be hired unnecessarily. It is key to remember: "Never hire staff to plug holes in the dike."

The time invested in reviewing your practice will have long-term benefits. "Improving or altering each step in the patient flow process can produce long-lasting results in patient satisfaction and in maximizing revenues."[4] Remember, if you review your operations and find that everything is working well, leave it alone. Keep the adage "If it isn't broke, don't fix it" in mind.

Defining System Needs   It is important to reflect on the practices' needs before immediately selecting the automated systems to implement.

In today's managed care environment, medical practices require a great deal of sophisticated information to properly manage operations. Thus, the search for a new system should encompass looking for the information required to manage the medical practice.

The most common approach to selecting a new system is to identify the weaknesses in the current system and try to fill in these gaps. The problem with this approach, however, is that the practice can miss valuable opportunities to revamp or enhance present operations if it is simply looking for stopgaps to fix inadequacies in the current system.

The information that the practice should have readily available in its information system can be defined in two broad categories (the reports listed here are a sample of the options available):

1. **Financial Accounting Reports.** These include:
   - *Accounts payable*: a listing of expenses that have been paid
   - *Balance sheet*: a statement of practice assets and liabilities
   - *Income and expense statements*: a report of revenue and expenses for the current period and a comparison of a previous period

2. **Managerial Accounting Reports.** These include:
   - *Accounts receivable management reports*:
     a. Aged analysis of accounts receivable
     b. Aged analysis of accounts receivable by payor
     c. Procedure analysis by the CPT® medical code and order of volume
     d. Diagnosis analysis
     e. Production report by doctor and/or other provider
     f. Referring physician analysis
     g. Miscellaneous reports designed for the practice and a report generator
     h. Scheduling reports, including:
        - Patient lag time between call and appointment
        - No-show report
        - Appointment reminder calls
        - Office waiting time between arrival and visit
     i. Demographic reports on patients
     j. Managed care reports for contract management, including:
        - Utilization report: charges to collections
        - Cost of providing services
        - Capitation profitability

Selection Process   Typically, computer systems in medical practices were selected for a single purpose: billing. Unfortunately, today's health care environment dictates more sophisticated requirements for the medical practice than an electronic billing system that simply prints claims forms and may or may not transmit electronic insurance claims. To successfully manage a medical practice in the current health care environment, it is necessary for a practice to have a versatile practice management system.

Modern technology has significantly improved practice management information systems over the past few years to meet the demands of managed care and other changes in the industry. The wide acceptance of patient scheduling, electronic claims submission, and increased interest and demand for electronic medical records have pushed software vendors to make major strides in their offerings. This factor, coupled with advances in hardware and reduction in cost, has fueled major changes in the products on the market.

The first step in determining the information system needs for your practice is to jot down the critical goals you want to accomplish with an electronic system. Following are a few sample goals that the practice may wish to expand upon:

1. Select a leading vendor that will still be in business in 5 years.

2. Include functional areas for the changing industry (ie, managed care, electronic medical records, office scheduling).

3. Establish a realistic timeline.

4. Implement a rough budget.

The second step is to develop a document that can be used as a *request for information* (RFI) and/or a *request for proposal* (RFP). The purpose of this document is to collect consistent data that can be compared for decision-making.

It is of paramount importance that the office staff is involved in this process and that they are encouraged to include elements that would not only enhance their work but also complement the manual systems that currently exist in the medical practice. The document should be created in sections that focus on specific aspects of the practice. A document of this nature not only is important in obtaining quotes but also focuses everyone's attention during system demonstrations.

Once the document is created, the practice should select several practice management system vendors and contact their marketing representatives. (See Appendix A for a list of the leading health care system vendors in the marketplace today.) The practice should share the selection document with the vendors to ensure that their systems can meet your requirements. Those that can should be invited to demonstrate their product to the office staff. The number of vendors selected should be limited to three to five or the process can become cumbersome, time-consuming, and ineffective.

It is critical to remember that an electronic system must fit the practice, not vice versa. Do not allow marketing representatives to sell you something that resembles placing a square peg in a round hole.

A demonstration should be established at the practice site for each of the selected vendors. Each member of the office staff should have a copy of the selection document and should independently evaluate each of the systems that are reviewed. Upon completion of the review process, all of the staff evaluations should be reviewed and tabulated. The vendors whose systems meet all or the majority of the criteria should then have an opportunity to bid on the system.

As a part of the final review process, each vendor should be requested to supply a list of references. It is imperative that these references be contacted without the marketing representative present. The individual making the reference calls should have a specific list of questions. And, if possible, he or she should visit the office of reference to speak with the staff members using the system. In addition, the office staff member conducting this process should review the system manuals that are provided by the vendor to see if they are easy to use and understand.

If all of the systems reviewed have similar pricing and features, the review then needs to go to the next level. The reviewer must have a second checklist in order to ask consistent questions for comparison. These questions should focus on system downtime, telephone support availability, support response time to calls, and other questions or concerns. (Appendix B contains a sample selection evaluation form to use when choosing between various physician practice management systems.)

After the completion of a thorough review process, the practice should have eliminated some of the competitors in the process. It is suggested that the process lead to two finalists in the bidding competition. In "Selecting Practice Management Information Systems," Robin Worley and Vincent Ciotti suggest that both of the finalists in the process be aware of the competitive bidding to afford the practice strong negotiating clout.[5] The authors further state:

- Involving end users heavily in evaluating systems not only gains their detailed input on features but also increases their "buy in;"

- Structured checklists can make steps such as telephone references and site visits as quantifiable as any RFP score;

- Perusing user manuals not only avoids marketing hyperbole but also serves as an excellent product definition for the contract; and

- Keeping two vendors in the running at the end, rather than having a single RFP winner, greatly increases negotiating clout.

Taking Bold New Steps

The business world has rapidly advanced into an environment rich in electronic technology, yet the business side of medicine has not kept pace. A quantum leap for medical practices is to implement and utilize electronic medical records. This can be an exciting, yet challenging, change. Over the past several years, electronic medical record technology has vastly improved and the cost of these systems has been decreasing. Thus, making the adoption of an electronic medical record more desirable and realistic.

Electronic Medical Records

Practice efficiencies can be greatly enhanced through the implementation of an electronic medical record system. In "Choosing and Implementing a Reliable Electronic Patient Record System," Patty Edwards-Capella states, "To gain the full benefits of an EPR [enterprise-wide patient record] system, it is important to first ensure efficient and cost-effective work processes are in place."[6] Thus, an electronic medical record system can only be instituted and used effectively if the practice has been reviewed and modified to enhance operations. Pope states this is a team effort. The doctor and staff must work closely together through the planning, contracting and implementation stages.

Halich, a practice information technology specialist in Identifying Practice Needs Before You Select An EMR, states many physicians don't want to spend time selecting an electronic medical record (EMR) system when one has been highly recommended by another practice. . . . You are more likely to be satisfied with an EMR that fits the specific needs of your practice, as it's critical that you identify these needs and determine how they will be met by the proper EMR system selection and implementation. She offers the following steps:

1. Identify clinical and administrative leaders who will sponsor and support the system selection and implementation effort. If it is a small practice make sure the office manager is on board with the concept.

2. Identify goals you would like to achieve.

3. Review and document your current clinical and administrative processes related to the use of an EMR.

4. Align your goals with the process improvement you identified to determine your system requirements (Halich, MGMA e-Connexion, Issue 39, Sept 2003).

The use of an electronic medical record system can also bring tangible, intangible, and nonfinancial benefits to the practice. Table 2.1 lists the benefits of electronic medical records systems as summarized in the article, "Cost Justifying Electronic Medical Records."[7]

Table 2.1: Sample Benefits of Electronic Medical Records Systems

	Tangible Financial Benefits	Intangible Financial Benefits	Nonfinancial Benefits
Product Enhancement	• Reduction in chart pulls reduces labor cost in medical records department • Automated interfaces reduce labor costs for personnel involved in coding, billing, manually retrieving lab results, and referral coordination • Transcription costs • Malpractice premium lowered • Less dictation time, faster documentation of encounters • Improved charge capture, documenting home health management • Reduced nurse intake time • Faster billing reduces cash cycle, cuts receivable days • Document storage space costs reduced	• Scheduling of resources becomes more efficient • Easier QA and UR reporting • Less time spent copying, filing, faxing, and transmitting data • Lower supply costs • Fewer lab results lost, fewer repeat tests • Aggregate patient data improves financial forecasting, risk assumption • Automation of referral process and more appropriate use of specialists	
Quality of Care Improvements	• Automated protocols/guidelines reduce expensive variations in patient treatment • Less time needed to search through records for relevant patient information • Decrease in lost lab reports reduces cost of repeat lab tests	• Reduced medication errors, adverse drug interactions • Improved primary and preventive care (through automated reminders, protocols, and alerts) reduces disease management costs, specialty, and inpatient care • Availability of chart vastly improved • Improved data analysis, outcomes measurement, population-based care • Remote access to patient charts • Summary screen helps prevent overlooked patient information • Ease of providing summary information helps specialists with care	• Improved quality of documentation • Improved outcomes reporting • Less information falls through the cracks in a continuum of care

	Tangible Financial Benefits	Intangible Financial Benefits	Nonfinancial Benefits
Improved Customer Service Satisfaction		• Less need for repeat lab testing • Ease of getting medication refills authorized; faster turnaround time on refill requests • Less paperwork as patients move throughout the health care system	• Confidence physicians are using the best information technology available • Improved communication with preformatted letters, educational handouts, etc.
Increased Professional Satisfaction	• More time to spend with patients	• Reduction in paperwork • Improved communication and less time consumed with routine information exchange	• Increased satisfaction with availability, documentation of records, efficiency of chart reviews and signing, etc. • Ease of covering for other providers' patients • Ease of tracking referred patients

Electronic medical records are a newer innovation when compared to other aspects of practice management systems. Making the correct choice for the practice will have significant long-range implications.

For example, some electronic medical record systems are now available online at a nominal cost. The online systems carry with them a concern for confidentiality and security of critical medical records information; however, it is apparent that some of these systems have an excellent security system and are worthy of consideration. Online systems bring with them a significant cost savings and require no major capital outlays to become operational.

In "Choosing and Implementing a Reliable Electronic Patient Record System," Patty Edwards-Capella offers the following 10 guidelines to follow when choosing an electronic medical records system, which are of paramount importance in planning and implementing an electronic medical records system that will be both productive and cost-effective[8]:

1. **Process Improvement**. For an electronic medical record system to function effectively, the practice must have accomplished all of the

requisite tasks and changes required from the re-engineering and process improvement discussed earlier in this chapter.

2. **Full On-Site Planning and Implementation Support.** Vendor selection is critical to the success of the project. After a careful planning process is completed, the process will require ongoing competent technical support.

3. **Modular, Scalable Design**. The implementation process should be gradual and eventually cover the entire practice. By being modular, the system you select will enable this type of growth process.

4. **Open, Nonproprietary Architecture**. The system should be based on industry standards and enable easy integration with various information systems.

5. **Customizable Workflow**. The system must have the capability to be modified to accommodate the practice workflow.

6. **Customizable Security**. Pick a system that enables the user to modify security and limit access to various applications.

7. **Electronic Data and Scanned Document Support.** The system must have the capability of incorporating both paper-originated and electronic data.

8. **Remote Access/Physician Office Integration**. The system should provide access to remote users.

9. **Health Care Dedication/Proven Record.** Follow the process earlier in this chapter regarding making reference checks.

10. **Applications to Improve Efficiency.** Ideally the system will contain applications designed to automate specific work processes and improve efficiencies, therefore aiding in cost containment.

The electronic medical record system, as a component of the practice management system, must interface with all of your other electronic systems in your practice. The system must work within the constraints of the practice and must complement the manual systems that are currently in place. The system, if utilized properly, can reduce costs, increase physician productivity, and enhance quality of patient care. Table 2.2 offers a list of several practice management software companies.

Table 2.2: Practice Management Software Companies

Rank	Company	Web site
1	McKesson Corp.	www.mckesson.com
2	WebMD Practice Services Inc.	www.medicalmanager.com
3	Cerner Corp.	www.cerner.com
4	NDCHealth Corp.	www.ndchealth.com
5	IDX Systems Corp.	www.idx.com
6	Per-Se Technologies	www.per-se.com
7	MEDITECH	www.meditech.com
8	Misys Healthcare Systems	www.misyshealthcare.com
9	EPIC Systems Corp.	www.epicsystems.com
10	CPSI	www.cpsinet.com
11	Companion Technologies	www.companiontechnologies.com
12	A4 Health Systems	www.a4healthsys.com
13	Athenahealth Inc.	www.athenahealth.com
14	VantageMEd	www.vantagemed.com
15	HealthVision	www.healthvision.com
16	NextGen Healthcare Information Systems	www.nextgen.com
17	Physician Micro Systems Inc.	www.pmsi.com
18	Greenway Medical Technologies Inc.	www.greenwaymedical.com
19	PracticeOne	www.practiceone.com
20	Antek Healthware Inc.	www.antekhealthware.com

Source: Phelps Research

Electing to convert to an electronic medical record system has some significant financial implications. The best method to review the costs and savings of an electronic medical record system is to develop a simple worksheet
that lists the cash outlays for the new system and the cost savings that will
be gained over a period of time. It is important to understand that implementing a new system will not have an immediate reduction in overhead,
but that over a period of time the practice will gain this benefit.

Following is a worksheet that can be used to calculate the overall cost and savings of the system. (This is a step that can be delegated to an office manager.)

Cost Savings Analysis for Electronic Medical Records

Expenditure

Hardware   _____

Software   _____

Estimated 5-year cost   _____

Cost Reduction

Staff reduction   _____

    File clerk   _____

    Transcriptionist   _____

Supplies no longer needed   _____

Estimated 5-year saving   _____

Increased Physician Productivity

(Number of additional encounters
× average revenue) × 5 years   _____

Net Financial Gain to Practice

Expenditure   _____

Less Cost Reduction   _____

    Sub-total   _____

    Plus increased production   _____

Automated Telephone Systems

Earlier in this chapter we discussed automated telephone systems. Many people have a negative reaction to placing a telephone call and having it answered by an automated attendant. But, from a management perspective, it can be a great asset to the practice and the patients. A system that is properly designed and managed can prevent frustrating busy signals for patients, properly direct the calls to the most appropriate individual, and allocate work loads to the entire office staff.

The simplest approach to selecting the appropriate automated telephone system for your office is to find the right vendor for your needs. The selected vendor should be presented with an RFP that lists all of your current needs and anticipated future growth. If the practice is not comfortable with this approach, one or more vendors should be asked to conduct a *needs analysis* of the practice and make recommendations with regard to one or more appropriate systems. Remember, as with anything else you purchase, a vendor will try to sell its best product with all the "bells and whistles." In most instances, the practice will not require all the sophisticated add-ons to the system. All the practice needs is a system that meets your basic needs to provide service to your patients and an effective tool for your staff.

What Makes It Work?

Two-way communication is the basic building block of sound management practices. Always tell your employees what you are trying to accomplish and how they will be a part of this change. The employees may have excellent ideas for modifying manual systems and about application issues for a new practice management information system.

How does a practice make all these changes and make them work? The most basic element of successfully managing the change process is to make all of the practice employees a part of the process. Meaningful involvement in re-engineering and process improvement builds a team that develops consensus and ownership in the changes that evolve. Many people are fearful of changes in their environment because something new can create anxiety and concern. Therefore, encouraging and insisting on participation in the development and implementation of changes help makes employees better understand the reason for change and encourage them to offer input and insight.

As the practice creates or modifies new manual systems, it is imperative that step-by-step procedures be documented for the new system. These procedures are necessary for training the staff and ensuring that each new employee who joins the practice will follow the same protocol. It is of critical importance that, as the manual systems are finalized, the practice constantly trains, retrains, and reassess. Never assume that everyone understands the procedure and how it is to be followed.

Endnotes

1. Conomikes G. *Conomikes Report on Medical Practice Management and Managed Care.* 18(1):4, 5; 98.

2. Conomikes G. *Conomikes Report on Medical Practice Management and Managed Care.* 18(1):4, 5; 98.

3. Boden TW. Study office flow patterns to avoid bottlenecks in your new design. *Physician's Advisory.* February 2000;(2):9, 10.

4. Dunevitz B. Maximize resources by re-engineering your medical group's patient flow process. MGM *Update.* February 15, 2000;39(4):1, 6.

5. Worley R, Ciotti V. Selecting practice management information systems. MGM *Journal.* May/June 1997;44(3):55-56, 58, 60, 62, 64-65, 78.

6. Edwards-Capella P. Choosing and implementing a reliable electronic patient record system. *Healthcare Informatics.* March 1998;15(3, Suppl): 3-5.

7. Renner K. Cost justifying electronic medical records. *Healthcare Financial Management.* October 1996.

8. Edwards-Capella P. Choosing and implementing a reliable electronic patient record system. *Healthcare Informatics.* March, 1998;15(3, Suppl): 3-5.

9. Pope, C. Group practices identify, overcome EMR barriers. MGMA *e-Connexion,* January 2005:5(1)

10. Halich, L. Information Management: Identify practice needs before you select an EMR, *MGMA e-Connexion,* September 2003:3(9).

11. Schryver, D. Re-engineering Group Practice Operations, MGM *Journal,* March 2001:48(2).

12. Nelson, R. Practice Management Systems: There must be a better way! *Directions* newsletter, 2003:5(2)

13. Lowes, R. Technology Consultant: Why not lease your computers?, *Medical Economics*, Jun 4, 2004:81(11), p17.

14. Wood, S. Know Your Business Model Before Choosing an IT System, *Behavioral Health Management*, Jan/Feb 2004:24(1), p45–48.

Chapter 3

Getting the Right People for the Job

Ohe of the most important factors in ensuring success for physician practices is the recruitment and retention of good employees. *Good employees* are associates who can help create a positive work culture, help provide quality health care, and help to contain costs.

Recruiting "Good" Employees

In *Human Resource Management: An Experiential Approach*, John Bernardin and Joyce Russell note that real-world organizational staffing is replete with examples of ineffective and/or inferior methods of recruiting personnel.[1] One of the best ways for physicians to contain costs is to pay special attention to recruiting and retaining personnel who fit best within their work culture.

Determining the Work Culture

Before the recruitment process can begin, physicians must first determine what type of work culture they hope to establish and understand their own values and the values of those they are seeking to employ. To help in this determination, physicians may wish to consult and/or use standardized tools. For example, one appropriate tool is Rudolf Moos' Work Environment Scale, which consists of 90 true and false statements in addition to an assessment of 10 "environmental dimensions" such as involvement, peer cohesion, supervisor support, autonomy, task orientation, and work pressure.[2]

Another helpful tool is Milton Rokeach's Value Survey, which has the respondent rank in order 18 instrumental and 18 terminal values.[3] Rokeach's Value Survey could be used when attempting to assess whether potential employees possess values desired in the physician's practice. The survey could also be used in interviews whereby the applicant could expand on his or her answers in the interview.

Establishing Job Descriptions

It is best to establish job descriptions that delineate what jobs, activities, behaviors, and duties are expected of an employee. Bernardin and Russell note that identifying the critical knowledge abilities, skills, and other characteristics (or KASOCs) is crucial when developing job descriptions, as these job descriptions will assist physicians and/or medical office managers in determining how the work gets completed and by whom.

Methods of Recruitment

Once the physician practice identifies jobs that need to be filled, the recruitment process begins. Some of the more common methods for recruiting personnel include newspaper advertising; visits to high schools, community colleges, and universities; notices to professional associations; referrals; and posting job positions to the Internet.

Job advertisements should always specify the minimum educational and experience requirements. Once a pool of candidates is identified, physician practices should have potential employees complete an application and any other appropriate information release forms. (See the following sidebars for a sample application for employment and a sample disclosure statement and release form.) It is also suggested that reference and/or background checks, as well as perhaps a standardized test and a structural interview, be required of all finalists.

Assistance in creating job descriptions can be obtained from colleagues, consultants, national training and certifying organizations, and various manuals such as David Jay's, The Essential Personnel Sourcebook[4] *and W. R. Lawsons'* How To Develop a Personnel Policy Manual.[5]

Sample Application for Employment

To the applicant: *[Practice Name]* is an equal opportunity employer and complies with all applicable federal, state, and local laws. No question on this application is used for the purpose of limiting or excusing any applicant from consideration for employment on a basis prohibited by local, state, or federal law.

PLEASE PRINT

Position(s) applied for _____ Date of application _____

Name _____ Social Security # _____

Address _____

City _____ State _____ Zip _____

Telephone # _____ Other phone # _____

Are you 18 years of age or older? _____ Yes _____ No
(If under 18, applicant will be required to submit a birth certificate or work
certificate as required by state and/or federal law.)

Have you ever been terminated for other _____ Yes _____ No
than economic reasons?

If yes, please explain _____

Have you ever been convicted of, or pleaded guilty or _____ Yes _____ No
no contest to, a crime in the last seven (7) years?

If yes, please explain _____

Do you have the legal right to work in the _____ Yes _____ No
United States?
(Successful applicants will be required to prove identity and eligibility of
employment.)

Driver's license number if driving is an essential job function:

_____ State: _____

Type of employment desired: Full-time _____ Part-time _____

Date available _____

SKILLS AND QUALIFICATIONS
Summarize any training, skills, licenses, and/or certificates that may qualify you for the job for which you are applying.

_____

_____

_____

_____

EDUCATIONAL BACKGROUND
Proof of education and training may be required upon employment.

Name and Location	Years Completed	Did you graduate?	
High School/GED			Course of Study
_____	_____	___ Yes ___ No	_____
College or University			Major/Degree
_____	_____	___ Yes ___ No	_____
Additional Schooling			Major/Degree
_____	_____	___ Yes ___ No	_____

EMPLOYMENT HISTORY
Provide the following information for your past four (4) employers, assignments, or volunteer activities, starting with the most recent.

_____ _____   _____   _____
From   To   Employer   Telephone

_____   _____
Job Title   Address

_____   Summarize the nature of work performed and
Immediate Supervisor and Title   job responsibilities

_____
Reason for leaving

_____   _____ _____   _____ _____
Hourly Rate/Salary   Start $ per   Final $ per

From	To	Employer	Telephone

Job Title   Address

Immediate Supervisor and Title   Summarize the nature of work performed and
                                   job responsibilities

Reason for leaving

Hourly Rate/Salary   Start $ per   Final $ per

From	To	Employer	Telephone

Job Title   Address

Immediate Supervisor and Title   Summarize the nature of work performed and
                                   job responsibilities

Reason for leaving

Hourly Rate/Salary   Start $ per   Final $ per

From	To	Employer	Telephone

Job Title   Address

Immediate Supervisor and Title   Summarize the nature of work performed and
                                   job responsibilities

Reason for leaving

Hourly Rate/Salary   Start $ per   Final $ per

REFERENCES

Please give the name of three persons not related to you, whom you have known for at least one year.

Name	Address	Years Known	Telephone #
1.			
2.			
3.			

EMPLOYMENT APPLICATION CERTIFICATION

I certify that this application was completed by me. I certify that the information in my application, in my resume, and in my interviews is true, complete, and correct. I understand that falsification or omission, whenever or however discovered, may jeopardize my opportunities for employment or, if hired, may be reason for termination of employment. While this application will be given every consideration, its receipt does not imply or guarantee that I will be employed.

If hired, in consideration of my employment, I agree to adhere to the policies and procedures of [*Practice Name*]. I understand that employment is for an indefinite duration and is terminable at will by either [*Practice Name*] or myself and that this application does not constitute a contract of employment.

I also understand and agree that the at-will nature of this employment can only be modified by written agreement between parties. I understand that no manager or representative other than the President/CEO (or assigned designee) has any authority to enter into any agreement for employment for any specified period of time or to make any agreement contrary to the foregoing.

I further understand that any offer of employment tendered as a result of this application is contingent upon successful completion of the following: a pre-employment post-offer drug screen, a fitness-for-duty assessment, verification of legal right to work in the United States, previous employment history, history of arrest and conviction, verification of education, professional licenses and certifications, personal references, and motor vehicle records.

By signing this application, I authorize [*Practice Name*] and its agents to investigate information I have given in this application, resume, or during the interview process and to conduct a background investigation. I hereby release all claims against [*Practice Name*] and its respective employees, officers, trustees, agents, and any person or agent supplying information that might arise out of the aforementioned investigation. I have received a "Disclosure Statement—Notice to Applicant of Intent to Obtain a Consumer Report." I have signed a "Release to Procure a Consumer Report."

This application when completed and signed becomes the property o
Name].

_____   _____

Applicant's Signature   Date

_____

Applicant's Name (Please Print)

Performing Reference and Background Checks

It is imperative that reference and/or background checks be conducted for each new employee you are considering hiring. At least three references should be checked by requesting either a letter or telephone interview that discusses the applicant's job history and skills. The primary reason for conducting checks is to ensure that the applicant's data are reliable and also to obtain the perceptions of previous employees or teachers regarding the employee's own record.

Bernardin and Russell also note that fear of negligent hiring is a related reason employers conduct checks of reference and background. In *Human Resource Management: An Experiential Approach*, Bernardin and Russell cite an example of an HMO that was sued for $10 million when a patient under the care of a psychologist was committed to a hospital and it was later revealed that the psychologist not only was unlicensed but also lied about his previous experience.[6] Attempting to accelerate the hiring process by forgoing prudent screening could cost more in the long run.

Another reason to check references is to attempt to ascertain if the potential hire will be able to succeed and grow into the job and contribute to the work environment in a positive manner. Physicians must recognize that each member of their practice plays an integral role in the profitability and success of the practice.

Bernardin and Russell also state that background checks should include police records, particularly convictions, and driving records, if applicable. If physicians are uncomfortable with letters of reference, which tend to be mostly positive, Bernardin and Russell advocate constructing a "letter of reference," or a recommendation that is essentially a performance appraisal form. They also suggest constructing a rating form and requesting that the evaluator indicate the extent to which the candidate was effective in performing a list of job tasks.

Although it appears to be cumbersome, physicians and/or medical office managers should attempt to do their best in obtaining valid reference checks. As Bernardin and Russell note, a good-faith effort to obtain verification of employment history can make it possible for a company to avoid (or win) negligent hiring lawsuits.

Conducting Interviews

The employment interview is still the most utilized tool for selecting employees. Following is a list of suggestions offered by Bernardin and Russell to help physicians and/or office managers conduct meaningful, effective employment interviews:

1. Exclude traits that can be measured by more valid employment tests, such as intelligence, job attitudes or ability, job skills, or knowledge.

2. Include motivational and interpersonal factors that are required for effective job performance. These two areas seem to have the most potential for both overall and interviewer validity. Interviewers should assess only those factors that are specifically exhibited in the behavior of the applicant during the interview and are critical for performance in the job to be filled.

3. Match interview questions (content areas) with the job analysis data of the job to be filled and the strategic goals of the organization.

4. Avoid biased language and jokes that may detract from the formality of the interview, and inquiries that are not relevant to the job in question.

5. Limit the amount of preinterview information to complete about the applicants' qualifications and clear up any ambiguous data. While knowledge of test results, letters of reference, and other sources of information can bias an interview, it is a good strategy to seek additional information relevant to applicants' levels of KASOCs. (See "Establishing Job Descriptions" earlier in this chapter for a definition of KASOC.)

Sample Disclosure Statement and Release Form

Notice to Applicant of Intent to Obtain a Consumer Report

By this document, [*Practice Name*] discloses the following to you. A consumer report may be obtained for employment purposes as part of the pre-employment background investigation and at any time during your employment.

> *A consumer report may include driving records, criminal arrests and convictions, prior employment history, verification of education, professional licenses and certifications, and other public record information.*

Before we may procure a consumer report, you must authorize such procurement in writing. You have the right to decline authorization for us to procure a consumer report. However, we will not consider you further for employment if you so decline.

On an attached form, you will find a release that will allow [*Practice* Name] to obtain a consumer report. Please read the release carefully before signing it and indicating your choice regarding disclosure.

Release to Procure a Consumer Report

I have read the "Notice to Applicant of Intent to Obtain Consumer Report" letter. I understand that I have the right to decline authorization for [*Practice Name*] to procure a consumer report concerning me.

I understand that the consumer report may contain information concerning criminal arrests and convictions, driving records, prior employment history, verification of education, and professional licenses and certifications.

I understand that, if hired, this authorization shall remain on file and shall serve as an ongoing authorization to procure consumer reports at any time during my employment period. Therefore, understanding these rights,

I (circle one) <u>AUTHORIZE / DO NOT AUTHORIZE</u> [*Practice Name*] to procure a consumer report concerning me.

_____

Applicant Name (Please Print)

_____   _____

Signature   Date

_____

Human Resources Representative

Many interviews are unstructured. These are usually characterized by open-ended questions that are not based on or associated with the job. However, research illustrates that structured interviews can improve the reliability and validity of the process.

Elaine Pulakos and Neal Schmitt studied experience-based and situational interviews in "Experience-Based and Situational Interview Questions: Studies of Validity."[7] They define experience-based interviews in which questions are *post-oriented* in that they ask the respondents to relate what they did in past jobs or life situations that is relevant to a particular job—relevant knowledge, skills, and abilities of successful employees. For example, "Think about a time when you had to motivate an employee to perform a job task that he or she disliked but that you needed the individual to do. How did you handle the situation?"

A situational interview question asks the job applicant to imagine a set of circumstances and then indicate how he or she would respond in that situation; hence, the questions are *future-oriented*. For example, "Suppose you were working with an employee who you knew greatly disliked performing a particular job task. You were in a situation where you needed this task completed, and this employee was the only person available to assist you. What would you do to motivate the employee to perform the task?"

Pulakos and Schmitt found that the experience-based interviews were more valid than the situational interviews under their tightly controlled experimental conditions. However, research suggests that using structured interviews rather than unstructured interviews obtains results with better reliability and validity.

Employees must also have the skills for the job and they must be encouraged to continue their education on the job. Bernardin and Russell acknowledge that companies are interested in selecting employees not only who will be effective, but who will also work as long as the companies want them, and who will not engage in counterproductive behavior, such as violence, substance abuse, avoidable accidents, and employee theft.

Personnel may account for a major portion of the physician office budget, but it is the personnel that are essential for the long-run success of any physician practice. Therefore, while it might seem cumbersome, it is crucial that time and money are allocated to recruit and retain the best employees.

Today's work environment has numerous employers competing for employees who can help make or break a practice.

Endnotes

1. Bernardin J, Russell J. *Human Resource Management: An Experiential Approach, Second Edition.* Boston, MA: Irwin/McGraw-Hill; 1998.

2. Moos R. *Work Environmental Scale Manual.* Palo Alto, CA: Consulting Psychologists Press; 1994.

3. Rokeach M. *Rokeach Value Survey.* Palo Alto, CA: Consulting Psychologists Press; 1988.

4. Jay D. *The Essential Personnel Sourcebook, Second Edition.* London, UK: Financial Times Management; 1998.

5. Lawson WR. *How to Develop a Personnel Policy Manual.* New York: AMACOM; 1998.

6. Bernardin J, Russell J. *Human Resource Management: An Experiential Approach, Second Edition.* Boston, MA: Irwin/McGraw-Hill; 1998.

7. Pulakos E, Schmitt N. Experience-based and situational interview questions: studies of validity, *Personnel Psychology*; 1995.

Chapter 4

Should You Purchase or Lease?

*D*r Brown resigned his position as a staff radiologist at Anywhere General Hospital and elected to open his own diagnostic imaging center. He met with his accountant and left the meeting more confused than he was when he went in. The accountant asked him a number of questions regarding financing the startup. Dr Brown had assumed he would use his personal savings as a downpayment and finance the balance. However, the accountant explained to Dr Brown that he could lease staff, real estate, and equipment, or he could hire employees directly and purchase the office building and the equipment. He explained the pros and cons of each scenario and asked Dr Brown to make a decision. Dr Brown left the accountant's office unsure of what decision to make.

Cost containment is a critical issue in medical practices facing declining revenue and increased operational costs. The decision to lease or purchase the practice facilities has a tremendous impact on the future overhead of any medical practice.

Starting a new practice, expanding an existing practice, or just replacing worn equipment and furnishing requires much greater analysis than would be expected. In the past, physicians wanting to accomplish any of the previously mentioned tasks could pick up the telephone, call his or her banker, and arrange a loan. That approach once worked, but in today's tumultuous health care environment a physician might be shocked at the response of the lending institution.

Many lenders are no longer the local banks with which the physician had a friendly relationship. Today, the physician often faces large conglomerates that follow strict rules and no longer employ "Mom and Pop" relationships as part of their banking strategies. As a matter of fact, new physicians entering practice for the first time may be surprised at the difficulty they face in borrowing money for their startup.

In addition to the complexities of borrowing money, physicians face perplexing issues related to hiring and managing staff for the practice. Most physicians are not trained in human resource management, may not know how to properly conduct interviews, and are usually unaware of the myriad state and federal regulations that must be followed in managing a staff of employees.

A fairly recent option that is available to physicians is *leasing* employees. This option and its consequences are discussed in this chapter. Remember: the decision to lease or purchase has significant long-range consequences that cannot be easily reversed. These consequences include federal and state tax implications that must be reviewed with the practice accountant.

Figure 4.1 provides a summary of the factors involved in making the "lease versus buy" decision, highlighting the key factors that play a role in this complex process.

Figure 4.1: A Summary of Factors Involved in Making the Lease versus Buy Decision

Selecting What You Want

The first step in deciding whether to lease or purchase the necessary equipment to run your practice is to decide what item the practice wishes to obtain and the specific brand that is desired. In order to accomplish this critical step, you must determine what features you want and exactly what you want the equipment to do.

The best place to start is to develop a *request for information* (RFI) and/or a *request for proposal* (RFP). This document can then be sent to three to five vendors. Once the vendors' responses are received, the practice should develop a spreadsheet so that all of the vendors can be compared feature by feature. When you have entered all of the responses to your RFI/RFP, you will easily be able to eliminate the vendors that don't meet your criteria.

The next step is to compare prices for each of the vendors that meet all of your preestablished criteria. You should then request a list of references from comparable practices that you can contact. Always contact the reference without the sales representative present. If the company representative insists on participating in the reference review, assume that they have something to hide and eliminate that vendor from your list of finalists.

Now, you are almost ready to make your selection. The last step is to review the financing aspect of your purchase. Most vendors will have leasing options available. Of course, you always have the option of making an outright purchase. This decision is the focus of our discussion.

When reviewing your options for the choice of equipment and the best price, make sure you also explore the purchasing cooperatives available to you. In many instances, local medical

This chapter focuses on cost containment and the factors that influence the financial viability of a medical practice. None of the authors is qualified to practice accountancy. Therefore, the purpose of mentioning these issues is to create awareness of issues that will have a significant impact on the viability of a medical practice. Prior to making decisions that have long-range financial implications, we strongly suggest you seek the advice of a qualified professional.

societies, medical specialty societies, independent practice associations (IPAs), hospital associations, chambers of commerce, and other groups have established purchasing alliances. Some of these purchasing alliances have arrangements with certain vendors for discounts on their products. These arrangements will take a lot of the hard work and research out of the purchasing process.

It is important to review warranties that are provided for the various items you are reviewing. Most of the warranties are similar, but they will not be identical. The terms of the warranties may be a key decision-maker.

Leasing Equipment

A good way to begin a discussion of leasing equipment is to review basic terminology. Leasing can be a confusing process that is filled with a language of its own.

Who's Who

The *lessor* is the party who owns the asset. The *lessee* is the party who rents the asset.

Types of Leases

There are two types of leases a physician may encounter: a capital lease and an operating lease.

- A *capital lease* is one in which the physician is planning a long-term commitment to utilize the asset, possibly for the life of the asset. This type of lease brings with it legal and accounting questions.

- An *operating lease* is utilized when an asset is needed on a short-term basis or the asset involves rapidly advancing technology that will render it obsolete in a relatively short time. The real question with an operating lease is how well you can negotiate advantageous terms.

Depreciation

Based on the advice of your accountant, leasing can be an excellent strategy for a medical practice. The key considerations involved in leasing are the availability of capital to make a purchase, the personal tax implications for the physician and for the practice as a business entity, and the long-range strategy that is being fulfilled. However, in addition to these issues, the physician must also consider depreciation.

Depreciation is the accounting and tax recognition of the decline in the value of an asset. It is an accounting number, not a cash flow. Depreciation expense offers a tax benefit to those who own assets; thus, a key factor in the decision to lease equipment is to weigh the tax benefit of utilizing depreciation versus writing off the lease payments.[1]

Conducting Due Diligence

In "Nine Things the Equipment-Leasing Salesman Won't Tell You," Milton Zall discusses some of the lesser-known facts of leasing[2]:

- Leasing isn't necessarily cheaper than buying.

- Any tax advantage will be outweighed by higher leasing costs.

- Leasing doesn't tie up your capital or credit line.

- You could be personally liable for fulfilling the lease.

- Leasing does not make your balance sheet look better.

- Leasing represents a commitment you may come to regret.

- The company may not like the condition of the equipment when your lease ends.

- The contract could contain a tax trap.

- The leasing company won't remind you when your lease expires.

Do these points mean that you should not lease because all leases are bad? No. Rather, the author points out that the leasing company is not looking out for the lessees' interests. Therefore, prior to entering into a lease, you should conduct a thorough due diligence process. This process begins by utilizing professionals, such as your accountant, to assist in determining the financial implications of leasing versus purchasing. In addition, legal counsel should review all lease documents prior to final execution of the document.

Financing

It cannot be emphasized enough that the financing option should match the use of the equipment being financed. If careful consideration is not given to all aspects of these choices, the practice may make some very costly mistakes. In "Analyzing Lease Purchase Options," an article that appeared in *Radiology Management*, David Cioleck and James Mace offer the following rules to guide the lease versus buy process[3]:

- Use the *purchase* alternative for assets that are certain to remain in the organization past their projected residual value life, without increasing the total cost of operation costs of retaining the asset to an unacceptable level.

- When the sole purpose is to preserve cash, but the same certainty of life within the organization exists as with the purchase alternative above, choose *finance* or *sales-type leases* (eg, $1 buyout, fixed balloon buyout, other fixed financing structures). Choose a lease term that is as well matched to the projected useful life as possible.

- If an identifiable term of use for the equipment is less than its full projected useful life, but preserving cash flow, limiting capital budgets, and keeping nonearning assets off the books are motivators, select a *fair market value lease* with an operating lease structure. However, choose a lease term to match how long it is projected to remain at your organization without major regard for the marketable life of the equipment.

- If uncertainty exists around the term of use within the organization or in the underlying technology of the equipment (rapidly changing technology), choose a *fair market value lease with a buyout range* (eg, a floor and a cap) or agreed upon renewal terms.

Office Space: Buy or Rent?

Buy

Many physicians in a private practice have a strong desire to own their office space. They believe that because they spend most of their working hours in the office, it would be better to own the space and not pay rent month after month. In most instances this is an emotional reaction that is not based on a financial analysis of this option.

Owning a medical office building may sound like an excellent strategy, but small commercial office buildings are not, in most cases, a good investment, as these properties can be difficult to rent or sell. The same funds invested in other financial instruments can yield a much higher return.

One of the key problems with a physician owning his or her own office building is that the physician is locked into an existing facility. The physician cannot make the building bigger if the practice grows and requires more space or, conversely, the physician cannot decide to use a much smaller space if he or she downsizes the practice. Linked to these issues is the fact that, over time, geographic areas change and the physician may want to move the practice or, even worse, the tenants decide to relocate because of population shifts or other related factors.

In today's environment many doctors use multiple sites for their practice. This means that a physician may only practice at a given location once or twice a week. It makes more sense to establish relationships with other physicians who can sublet the space, thereby reducing overhead, than to acquire the building and be locked into a situation that does not meet the needs of the practice.

Property management and ownership is a time-consuming and costly activity, and most physicians are too busy with their existing work schedules and personal lives to properly attend to it. Adding the significant responsibility of being a landlord will keep physicians from their patients and primary source of revenue, put physicians in a business where they most likely have no training or experience, and expose them to financial risk. If a physician is considering purchasing his or her office space, he or she should review this option carefully with professional advisors to weigh the personal and financial risks involved.

Rent

A majority of physicians lease office space, because it appears to be the simplest and most efficient way to begin or move a practice. In reality, the long-term office lease represents one of the most complex relationships in modern commerce.[4]

The first step in leasing office space is to determine a geographic area, where you wish to practice. This may sound extremely basic, but it requires some time and effort to make the right decision. Selecting a location will be very different for a sub-specialist whose practice is highly dependent on referrals and close proximity to a hospital, as opposed to a family practitioner with little or no hospital practice.

One of the best places to begin your search is with the medical staff office and/or administration of your local hospital. The hospital, most likely, has conducted extensive demographic studies of the market area. They will be able to tell you the geographic breakdown by age, sex, payor mix and physician needs. In addition, they have an extensive knowledge of available office space.

The second step is determining your exact space needs and the approximate configuration of the office layout. There are several options available to you in obtaining appropriate design assistance. Landlords may have architects they utilize, vendors will often provide space planning or you may copy a colleague's floor plan you admire. Be realistic in determining space needs. If you're planning to have an associate within one year you need to obtain the space at the onset or your lease. If an associate is a 3–5 year objective do not lease the space now.

The next step is to decide who can best assist you in negotiating the lease. If you have no experience there are several options available to you including relying on a professional commercial realtor, hiring a consultant and/or retaining a real estate attorney to review and negotiate the lease. We always recommend using legal counsel for the final review of the lease, due to the extensive financial and long-term commitment being made. If you do not have an attorney contact your local medical society for a referral.

Once you have selected a site and found an appropriate office space, you should submit a letter of intent to the lessor. In the letter of intent, and in greater detail in the lease itself, the following factors must be addressed: (1) rent; (2) renewal; (3) expansion rights; (4) improvement allowances; (5) deposits; (6) personal guarantees; (7) sub-leases and assignment; (8) construction; (9) default and termination provisions.[5]

As an aside, prior to beginning the search for an office, you should meet with your financial advisor, consultant and/or office manager to establish a budget for the new office. It is extremely important to determine exactly what you can afford to spend on the furnishings, improvements and monthly office rent. It is very common for physicians to move into a new office space and find financial planning has been less than adequate.

If your practice is operating and you want to move to a more desirable location or to a different office in your current building there are several things you can do to maximize the value you obtain in a lease:

1. Use time to your advantage.

2. Understand your options in the market.

3. Use your inside knowledge of your current building and/or landlord's operations to formulate the terms of your renewal deal.

4. Analyze your current lease for business and operational terms that have been inadequate, too costly, not operated as you expected and intended they might.

5. Let your landlord know you actively seeking alternative solutions for your space needs.

6. Understand what it will cost your landlord if you move out.

7. Be prepared to move if you can't get market rate terms.[4]

After payroll expense, rent is usually the highest single practice expense. Negotiating the best lease terms is critical to any physician trying to manage the ever escalating costs of a medical practice. There are some very significant hidden costs that may appear in lease clauses. Identifying theses issues and appropriately arranging favorable terms can save thousands of dollars over the life of a lease. These clauses include:

1. Real estate taxes—understand what is being passed through and if it is equitable.

2. Common area maintenance (CAM) and heating, ventilation and air-conditioning (HVAC) operating costs—Be sure you are aware of what your lease requires you to pay in terms of cleaning, security, maintenance and repairs, etc. Try to negotiate a fixed fee or cap on the amount.

3. Rent escalations—Rent tends to be fixed for one year at a time. Landlords insist on annual increases based upon the percentage increase in the Consumer Price Index (CPI). Try to prevent an increase for, at least, the first 2 years or try to establish a fixed amount for the increase.

4. Terms of the lease—Landlords are typically willing to make concessions for longer-term leases. For tenants, a longer-term lease has benefits and risks. The benefit is knowing the space is available at a predictable cost for the long-term. The risk is that the practice space needs may change and you may be locked into paying above market rent if demand for rentals subsequently declines. Try to negotiate a shorter term lease with renewal options, e.g., a two-year lease with four two year renewal options as opposed to a ten year lease.

5. Tenant improvements—Try to negotiate new paint and carpeting into the terms of the lease.

6. Repairs and replacement—Be aware of a clause that says at the end of the lease you have to return the premises in their original condition. Try to negotiate a clause stating you will return the space in original condition excluding wear and tear, unavoidable circumstances not your fault and alterations made with the approval of the landlord.

7. Assignments and subletting—New practices should negotiate enough flexibility to allow for mergers, sales and ownership changes.

8. Option to renew—Try to get this option established at a fixed, pre-determined rated not based on "fair market value."

9. Right of first refusal for additional space—This will obligate your landlord to show you vacant space as it becomes available before it goes to an outside party (www.allbusiness.com/articles/content/1041.asp).

Real estate leases are both long-term and financial commitments, which can have a significant role in the ultimate success of your practice. Be sure to carefully plan, review and negotiate these leases with extreme care, and we cannot over emphasize the importance of seeking professional advise before committing your signature and finances to a legal document of this nature.

Leasing Staff

Cost containment can be accomplished in various ways. One of the methodologies gaining significant attention is *outsourcing*. Outsourcing of various practice functions can help contain costs, even though it may not initially bring with it a reduction in cost. By outsourcing, the physician can focus on the primary business of patient care and allow others to deal with the complex management issues that abound in the practice. Outsourcing of various medical practice functions is not a new concept in the health care industry—hospitals have outsourced numerous functions, such as house-keeping, for many years.

The outsourcing function of interest in this discussion is *employee leasing.* Employee leasing has become a booming industry that targets small businesses, making physician practices a prime target. There are advantages and disadvantages to outsourcing your practice employees, and you should investigate this thoroughly before considering a major shift in the management of your practice.

Employee leasing is accomplished by retaining a firm that will "lease" the employees of the practice that hired them. The leasing firm, for a fee of about 2% to 8% of total payroll costs, assumes the human resource management and all associated personnel paperwork. The employee leasing firm will assume responsibility for payroll administration, benefit administration, unemployment compensation, and compliance with federal and state labor laws.

From the perspective of busy physicians, leasing staff makes it possible to reduce workload in an area that is almost always rife with problems. For all practical purposes, the physician retains management control of the staff and the employee leasing company retains control of the human resource functions. The doctor writes one check per month to the employee leasing firm and that organization assumes responsibilities for all payroll and employee benefit payments.

Jay Finegan, author of the *Inc.* magazine article "Look Before You Lease," offers some criteria for consideration when considering employee leasing:[6]

- Complete a due diligence process on the employee leasing company and be sure they are financially solvent.

- Request a long list of references and contact each one personally.

- Make sure you are comfortable with the employee leasing company.

- Be sure of the services that are available and that they meet your needs.

- Have the contract reviewed by legal counsel to ensure that the practice is amply protected.

The decision to lease employees is complex. First, the physician must be sure that this type of arrangement will blend with his or her management style and needs. Second, the physician must be sure that employee leasing makes financial sense for the practice. Third, outsourcing of services is not for everyone. Some physicians are content with only managing the clinical aspect of the practice, while others become extremely frustrated with dealing with an additional tier of management to accomplish tasks that were completely under their control in the past.

If employee leasing is a consideration, it is important to shop around for the best deal: one that accomplishes all of the practice goals and objectives, not necessarily the one that is the cheapest. Negotiate and get what you want or do not undertake employee leasing.

Negotiating Leases

Negotiating is a critical skill in the management of any business. In a medical practice that is diligently working toward financial success, negotiating becomes critical. From a cost containment perspective, a poorly negotiated lease can have a disastrous impact on the practice bottom line for years after the lease is signed. It is imperative that physicians culminate their search and negotiation with the best lease terms available.

Prior to starting the search for new equipment, or whatever is being leased, the physician should complete a due diligence process. This process should include the following:

- An understanding of what additional debt service the practice can manage on a monthly basis.

- A definition of what the practice specifically is trying to accomplish and why.

- A definition of the terms the practice willing to accept (such as 3, 5, or 10-year amortization of the note, small payments with a balloon payment at the end of the lease, a number of months with no payment, and so on).

- Assurances that the lease terms take seasonal fluctuations in patient volume and cash flow into consideration. Understand the life of the proposed equipment and make sure a lessor allows for upgrades of the equipment during the life of the lease.

- A review your own credit and the practice's credit. Make sure you know where you stand, because the strength of your credit will determine how good a deal is obtained and the strength of your negotiating position.

Compare Lessors

Once the basics have been mapped out, the practice is ready to begin shopping for leases. It is critical that a number of lessors be contacted and compared for the best rates and terms. Do not rely on the equipment vendor or manufacturer to provide the optimal leasing package.

The simplest way to compare lessors is to create a spreadsheet and compare the features of each financing option offered. This is a simple way of matching the features and terms of each lease by scanning your spreadsheet. This spreadsheet could be very simply taken to the next step and turned into an RFI or an RFP. The data obtained from these requests could then be plugged into the spreadsheet for comparative purposes.

It is important to remember that each financial organization will have variations in its leases. During your review of leases it is important to watch for hidden costs that have been placed in the lease.

Upon completion of your lease review, there is one more important step: *Do not accept the service agreement that is offered with an equipment lease*, as it will not always be the most comprehensive or cost-effective. Shop around for third-party vendor service agreements. The practice may be able to obtain a service contract for up to 35% to 60% less than those offered by the original equipment manufacturer.

During the due diligence process, there is nothing wrong in letting lessors know they are competing for your business. Never be afraid to ask for the terms you would like in the lease. In many instances, the lessor may be flexible in order to make a sale.

Review Documents

Finally, at the end of the negotiating process, the selected lessor will provide you with multiple documents for signature. It is extremely important that every document be carefully reviewed and fully understood prior to signing. It is also strongly recommended that the practice have legal counsel review these documents and offer suggested enhancements or changes. Often the attorneys' suggestions can be incorporated into the lease. There may also be times when a contract is so onerous that the wise decision is to say no and select a different lessor. Remember, if it sounds too good to be true, it probably is!

Purchasing

The decision to purchase equipment is somewhat simpler to carry out than the decision to lease. If you have decided to buy then you have eliminated the concerns associated with the complexities of leasing. But an astute buyer will look at numerous issues that apply to the buying cycle.

After deciding to buy a specific item, whether small or a capital purchase, the potential buyer must look at several critical issues, including the following:

- Should the purchase be for cash taken from operations or the physicians' personal savings?

- Should the purchase be financed through a loan to the practice?

- What about service contracts?

- Where do I go for the best deal?

Purchasing is a complex process that follows a similar format to leasing. In reality, the process that is followed should be identical to leasing, up to the point of paying for the purchase. As discussed earlier, you should go through a due diligence process and make a determination as to the best source of funds for you to utilize in making your purchase.

Decision Factors

There are several key factors that may slant the decision process to a buying scenario. The first of these factors, and probably the most important, is the impact on cash flow. It is important to review the lease or buy options and determine which will have the least negative impact on cash flow for the practice. This is accomplished by preparing a lease versus buy analysis chart. The bottom line of this analysis will reveal the best option.

Another critical issue in purchasing is to determine the potential value of the equipment after 5 years of use. If the equipment is worth more than 10% of the original purchase price, buying may be a viable option. Generally, a good rule of thumb is to not buy high-tech equipment or equipment that is evolving very rapidly. For example, it makes more sense to purchase x-ray equipment, which rarely makes major changes, than to purchase magnetic resonance imaging (MRI) equipment, where the technology is rapidly advancing and obsolescence is a constant reality.

The next issue for review is depreciation. In almost all instances, lessees are unable to depreciate the equipment they have leased. However, a buyer can fully depreciate the equipment over a period of time and expense the amount depreciated each year. It is important to have your accountant review this aspect of a purchase before you make a final decision.

Finally, when purchasing, the buyer must review the sales tax consequence and compare it to the taxes that are placed on a lease. Sales tax issues will vary from state to state; thus, it is important to have your accountant analyze the consequences of either decision.

The most widely used comparison is the lease versus purchase internal rate of return (IRR) produced by measuring the cash flow of the purchase case compared to the cash flow of the lease case.[7] The number that results is a measure of the rate of return of using your money for one scenario or the other. As the number gets higher, the concept of purchasing becomes more attractive. Figure 4.2 illustrates an example of a methodology that can be used for comparing two options that are available.

Figure 4.2: The After-Tax Purchase Comparison versus Leasing

Example Model: 3-Year Term						
Leasing Costs						
Initial purchase price		$1,000				

Purhase vs lease comparison	Rate	Initial Cost	Year 1	Year 2	Year 3	Total
Lease cost						
Base monthly lease cost w/use tax	6%	$1,000.00				
Annual leasing cost	0.02895		$368.24	$368.24	$368.24	$1,104.73
Taxes	38%		($139.93)	($139.93)	($139.93)	$419.80
Net annual leasing cost			$228.31	$228.31	$228.31	$684.93
Purchase cost						
Cost		$1,000.00	$0.00	$0.00	$0.00	$1,000.00
Book expenses						
Sales tax-capital	6.00%	$60.00				
Depreciation	3		$212.00	$339.20	$203.52	$754.72
Book (gain)/loss of sale			$0.00	$0.00	$235.16	$235.16
Taxes			($80.56)	($128.90)	($166.70)	($376.15)
After-tax purchase cost of funds	7.00%		$74.20	$59.36	$35.62	$169.18
Total initial cost		$1,060.00				
Net annual book expense			$205.64	$269.66	$307.59	$782.90
Net income impact						
Leasing cost			$228.31	$228.31	$228.31	$684.93
Purchase cost			$205.64	$269.66	$307.59	$782.90
Purchase vs lease book expense benefit			$22.67	($41.35)	$79.28	($97.96)
Cash flow impact						
Of leasing—annual leasing cost			($228.31)	($228.31)	($228.31)	($684.93)
Net cash flow of leasing		$0 00	($228.31)	($228.31)	($228.31)	($684.93)
Of purchasing						
Book expense			($205.64)	($269.66)	($307.59)	($782.90)
Add non-cash expenses—depreciation			$212.00	$339.20	$203.52	$754.72
Add non-cash expenses—gain/loss			$0.00	$0.00	$235.16	$235.16
Subtract non-book items—total initial cost		($1,060.00)	$0.00	$0.00	$0.00	($1,060.00)
Add sale of equipment proceeds			$0.00	$0.00	$70.13	$70.13
Subtract taxes on gain on sale					$0.00	$0.00
Net cash flow of purchase		($1,060.00)	$6.36	$69.54	$201.21	($614.81)
Cash flow impact of purchase vs lease		($1,060.00)	$234.67	$297.85	$429.52	($97.96)
Purchase payback		$1,060.00	$825.33	$527.48	$97.96	
Payback period (years)	3.2		1.0	1.0	1.2	
Net present value of purchase		0	1	2	3	
vs lease cash flow	–5.4%	($1,060.00)	$241.00	$324.00	$494.00	$0.00
Purchase vs lease IRR	**–5.47%**					

Endnotes

1. Bukics RM, Chambers, DR. *Medical Practice Accounting & Finance: A Practical Guide for Physicians, Dentists, and Other Medical Practitioners.* New York, NY: Probus Publishing; 1995.

2. Zall M. Nine things the equipment-leasing salesman won't tell you. *Physician's Management.* April 1998.

3. Cioleck D, Mace J. Equipment acquisition using various forms of leasing. *Radiology Management.* May/June 1998.

4. Goldstrom, D., Wournell, D. Heads Up! *A Guide To Negotiating Your Next Office Lease.* Canada: Northwest Publishers, 2003.

5. Reynolds, *Medical Economics.* May 2003: 80(9) p62.

6. Finegan J. Look before you lease. *Inc.* February 1997.

7. Cioleck D, Mace J. Analyzing lease purchase options. *Radiology Management.* May/June 1998.

8. Brannon, L. What You Should Know Before Signing an Office Lease. *Business Finance.* Jan 2005, 11(1), p16.

9. Negotiating An Office Space Lease. http://www.officespacesearchusa.com/negotiating-an-office-space-lease.htm

10. Negotiating The Best Lease Terms. http://www.allbusiness.com/articles/contnet/1041.asp

11. Napiewocki, J. Margin for Improvement? *Healthcare Financial Management.* Feb 2005: 59(2), p46-50.

12. More Hospitals Opting to Lease Equipment. *Hospital Materials Management.* Jul 2003: 28(7), p1.

13. Gans, D. On the edge: Following a road map to success. MGMA *Connexion.* Jul 2003: 3(6).

Chapter 5

Selecting and Working With Consultants

Good consultants can help increase productivity, provide innovative ideas and services, and cut or contain costs. They can help reduce paperwork, ensure compliance with various regulations, and help with staffing issues and concerns.

Hiring a Consultant

Following are six suggestions for working with consultants:

1. **Be proactive.** Line up help before you need it. Search out various consultants you need immediately and those you may need later.

2. **Start from the middle and work toward the top.** The difference between the "middle" and the "top" consultants may not be worth their differences in cost. Often, qualified, knowledgeable consultants looking to grow might be more cost-effective and practice attentive. That is, major problems and issues within the practice, if identified early, may not need high-priced, big-name consulting firms. (And often the work at the big names is handled by less senior personnel anyway.) Therefore, why pay for the embellishments of these high-priced consultants when others will do?

3. **Check and recheck references.** Be sure to ask for and check references. It is also important to check various regulating bodies and peer review groups when available to ensure the reliability and track record of any consultant.

4. **Communicate constantly with the consultant(s).** Let consultants know how the practice is progressing. Any major changes should be shared with the consultants.

5. **Always review and re-review the consultant's advice.** In most cases, advice should be followed, but if physicians find the advice unhelpful or detrimental they should not be afraid to speak with the consultant and, if needed, look for a replacement.

6. **Consultants work for the physician; not vice versa.** Be demanding and make clear what you expect. You are paying for the services of the consultant, so you should be satisfied with his or her work. The worst situation is to be unhappy or disappointed with a consultant and to not maximize efficiency and profitability.

In "Don't Ask the Questions if You Don't Want to Know the Answer," an article that appeared in *Physician Executive*, Daniel Zabel and Ronald Kaufman note that outside expertise is sought for one or more of the following reasons:

- The lack of "in-house" personnel or time to deliver a product.

- The need for an external expert to bring credibility to the project.

- Getting someone outside your organization to deliver unpopular or bad news.

- A genuine interest in the independent findings and recommendations of the consultant.

Zabel and Kaufman further note that "whatever the motivation for seeking the advice of outside counsel, be sure you are prepared for the answer they may give to the question you asked."[1]

Some of the experts physicians may need to consider consulting include bankers, accountants, attorneys, and health care consultants.

Consultants Checklist

Following is a checklist to use when selecting various consultants for your practice. It can provide a means to compare different consultants and help narrow the choices.

Chemistry: _____

_____

Education: _____

_____

Experience: _____

_____

Training: _____

_____

Philosophy: _____

_____

Resources: _____

_____

Areas of Interest: _____

_____

Professional and Community Involvement: _____

_____

Type and Size of Firm: _____

_____

Schedule: _____

_____

References: _____

_____

Honors/Awards: _____

_____

Value Survey: _____

_____

Experience-Based Situations: _____

_____

Bankers

Physicians and medical office managers should have at least one local banker, and they should consider retaining one or two national bankers. Often, bankers are one of the first professionals physicians consult because they can help in financing the physician practice. Bankers can establish lines of credit and can be a great vehicle for obtaining local business information and providing contacts.

Any additional cash should be employed in a high-yield money market account. Almost every newspaper lists the top yielding accounts each week. For example, Barron's, a financial weekly publication lists the top savings deposit yields each Monday. On April 25, 2005, Capital One money market account had a 3.10 percent rate with a 3.15 annual percentage yield. The Wall Street Journal publishes similar data from another financial source in its Wednesday edition in the Money and Investing section.

Accountants

Before selecting a certified public accountant (CPA) for your practice, it is important to do your research. The National CPA Health Care Advisors Association (www.hcaa.com) recommends researching the following criteria before selecting a CPA: expertise, education, training, resources, area(s) of concentration, professional and community involvement, size of the firm, price, chemistry, and references. For example, following are a few of the questions a physician should ask a CPA before making the decision to hire him or her:

- How many years' experience does the CPA have and with what type of health care clients?

- What degrees did the CPA earn?

- How much continuing professional education (CPE) did the accountant earn? When and where?

- Where did the CPE earn his or her credits in the past 5 years? How much work was in health care?

- Who does the CPA use for researching potential problems?

Physicians most often need CPAs who do a significant amount of work in health care. And, with all of the changes occurring in health care, physicians should know what CPAs do to stay abreast of changes. It is also important to know what, if any, professional and trade organizations the CPA belongs to. For example, is he or she a member of the National CPA Health Care Advisors Association, the Medical Group Management Association, American College of Health Care Executives, or the American College of Health Care Administrators? Physicians should also know what type of involvement and participation the CPA has in such professional organizations and the community. For example, does the CPA hold any leadership roles?

In addition, physicians must decide if they want to work with a sole practitioner or a CPA associated with a small, medium, or large firm. Physicians should also consider whether they need a regional, national, or international firm.

Physicians also must have the CPA explain the billing fees and procedures, which should be held in writing and provide answers to such questions as, when support staff is used will this be billed at a different rate? What are these rates?

One of the most important criteria in selecting and retaining CPAs is the chemistry between the CPA and the physician and the medical office manager. In addition to many of the criteria mentioned above, none of it will matter if the physician and CPA do not have a good working relationship. Poor chemistry can only result in an inefficient and costly relationship.

Physicians should review at least three CPAs before making their final selection, and those CPAs should have letters of reference from health care clients.[2] A good place to find potential CPAs is from referrals from friends, bankers, or other consultants, or seeking names from national groups such as the National CPA Health Care Advisors Association.

Attorneys

There are plenty of attorneys to choose from; however, physicians should be prudent about whom they select. Proper selection of attorneys has saved physicians and their practices thousands of dollars.

In *The Upstart Small Business Legal Guide, Second Edition,*[3] Robert Friedman suggests asking attorneys the following questions:

- What is your experience with the type of legal matter that I have?

- What are your initial consultation fee and hourly rates?

- Have you lectured at services held for the general public or other attorneys or written books or articles?

- How many attorneys are in your firm? Is it a full-service firm?

- What days and hours is the office open?

- Does the firm have specialists? If so, in what areas? (While in some states attorneys cannot hold themselves out as specialists, they may still state that their practice is "limited" to a certain area of the law, such as divorce, corporate, or criminal.)

- What percentage of your practice is devoted to my type of legal problem?

- Does the firm provide tax preparation and tax planning?

- Does the firm publish a client newsletter in which it explains new developments in the law? Are informational pamphlets on the law available?

- Is the attorney familiar with the following areas of federal and state law: income and estate taxation, corporation, aging, partnership, securities, antitrust, contracts, and product liability?

- Does the attorney have knowledge and experience with such nonlegal concepts as corporate finance, financial accounting, management technologies, and how to work with bankers, brokers, insurers, and industrial development agencies?

Friedman also discusses the importance of preventive legal audits (PLA). PLAs are comprehensive appraisals of a physician practice's legal affairs whereby attorneys can make constructive recommendations for changes in physician practice policies and procedures. Friedman states that annual PLAs can help clients do the following:

- Avoid jail and fines

- Avoid court

- Reduce legal costs

- Improve their reputation and public relations

- Take advantage of future trends

- Educate their employees

- Improve their work environment

According to Friedman, attorneys who conduct PLAs should visit a practice, analyze the practice's legal vulnerability, and draft a remedial plan for the client explaining potential legal exposure.[3]

Health Care Consultants

Physicians may also elicit the help of health care consultants to assess the practice's work environment and recommend ways for increasing the practice's organizational efficiency and effectiveness. Some of the best places for selecting consultants include:

- American Association of Healthcare Consultants (www.aahc.net)

- Medical Group Management Association (www.mgma.com)

- The Society for Healthcare Strategy and Market Development (www.stratsociety.org)

Physicians should follow the same steps that are used in selecting bankers, accountants, and attorneys, making sure to ask health care consultants for specific successful cases and turnaround situations.

Endnotes

1. Zabel D, Kaufman R. Don't ask the questions if you don't want to know the answer, *Physician Executive*. 1995.

2. American Association of Healthcare Consultants (www.aahc.net).

3. Friedman R. *The Upstart Small Business Legal Guide, Second Edition*. Chicago, IL: Dearborn Financial Publishing; 1998.

Chapter 6

Recruiting and Retaining Practitioners

The decision to add an additional practitioner to a practice can be a difficult one, and one that comes with significant cost considerations. Before making such a decision there are numerous issues to examine. And, once you have made the decision to add a practitioner, whether a physician extender or a full- or part-time physician, how you go about the process will also affect your costs. This chapter looks at the decision-making process and explores cost considerations inherent in the decision to increase staff.

Determining a Need for Additional Staff

There are many reasons for adding help to a practice. The most obvious is to handle a rising demand for medical services experienced by the practice. When patients must wait weeks or even months for an appointment, or when the practice will no longer accept new patients because of the demand of current patients, there is clear indication that the current system is overloaded, being run inefficiently, or not meeting the needs of the community. Both situations can signal the need to consider adding an additional practitioner. But there are other reasons to consider this step.

Help With Patient Volume

In some practices, senior physicians may wish to slow down and work limited schedules. Other physicians may wish to pursue opportunities both in and out of medicine that will require additional help with the patient volume. These, too, will require the addition of practitioners.

Creation of a Multispecialty Practice

At some point, the volume of referrals a practice makes to other physicians in a specific specialty may become great enough to warrant the addition of that physician or other provider to perform those services within the practice. It is not unusual for a busy practice to refer a significant number of patients for specific treatments or procedures not currently provided in the practice. In reviewing the referrals a practice makes to other physicians, an opportunity to retain those patients and the attendant revenue may exist, thereby expanding the scope of the services offered by the practice. This can be the beginning of a multispecialty practice.

Deciding to Add Staff

The decision to add staff to a practice should not be made lightly. The current practice operations should be carefully analyzed to determine whether such a move makes financial and practical sense. In addition, efficiency of operations should be evaluated. In many cases, changes in the practice's patient flow and scheduling may solve the demand for care. Analysis of unmet needs can also indicate alternatives to adding new staff. Don't jump to conclusions based on anecdotal information.

If, after careful review, it is apparent that the practice should consider adding a practitioner or other staff, the rest of this chapter can help determine the course of action and identify cost containment considerations for the process.

Adding Physician Extenders

The use of physician extenders—such as physician assistants and nurse practitioners—has increased in recent years for many reasons. Pressure from managed care organizations to increase access coupled with reduced reimbursement has been one factor. The need to provide care in medically underserved areas is another. The use of physician extenders in a practice also helps to maintain the necessary volume of all patients in a practice: with physician extenders, physicians are able to see patients with more serious medical conditions while physician extenders handle more of the routine care.

The decision to use a physician extender must be made carefully and only after a detailed analysis of the practice's needs and the role and limitation of the extender. If an extender can provide the care needed, the practice can see significant cost savings. In addition, the cost to recruit physician extenders is generally lower than that of a physician.

Types of Physician Extenders

There are several types of physician extenders working in physician practices throughout the United States. Some are trained in specific fields, such as optometrists (who may work in an ophthalmologist office to provide refractive services) or chiropractors (who may be hired by orthopedic surgeons to provide manipulation services). Others provide a broader range of patient services. It is this category of physician extenders that is seeing a great growth in demand. The two principal types of extenders in this category are physician assistants (PAs) and nurse practitioners (NPs).

PAs and NPs can provide a cost-effective means of expanding a practice's volume. However, care must be used to determine whether these extenders are able to provide the care needed to meet the demand for growth in the practice. To make this determination, you must look at the limitations of PAs and NPs and carefully analyze the services your practice is providing.

Limitation of Extenders

The care physician extenders can give is limited by several entities. The limitations may be created by state statutes, which regulate the practice of the extenders, and by third-party payors, who may specify limitations on reimbursement.

Before considering the use of physician extenders, carefully review the limitations. Start with the state law and regulations that identify the specific and general areas in which an extender can be used. Determine whether the laws in your state allow the use of physician extenders in the areas in which you wish to use them.

You may review the state laws yourself or contact the professional society for the particular

Separate laws govern PAs and NPs, and these laws vary between states. For example, only the state of Mississippi disallows the use of PAs in all practices except in federal facilities.

physician extender. These societies will be glad to inform you of the services that the extender can provide and under what circumstances.

It is also important to check with the various third-party payors for which you provide care to ascertain what services are covered and what the reimbursement will be. Some third-party payors may also impose additional limits on the use of extenders. Make sure you get this information in writing and seek any necessary clarification.

General Uses of Extenders

Physician extenders, including PAs and NPs, can practice in a variety of settings. Again, their roles may be limited by state law or by third-party payors, but generally, they work effectively in most outpatient settings including offices, clinics, nursing homes, and so on. They can perform physical examinations, order laboratory tests, diagnose and treat illnesses, suture wounds, and assist in surgery. Many states allow PAs and NPs to prescribe medications. It is important for each physician supervisor to determine what services he or she wishes his or her extenders to perform within the limit of the extenders' training and applicable state laws.

If your practice provides services in the areas in which physician extenders are capable of providing support, extenders may be a good option to handle the demand for more services.

Adding Physicians

Adding a new physician to your practice is the most costly option to handle the demand for patient services. However, if you have determined that adding a physician is the best option, you should be prepared to undertake a thorough analysis of your practice to determine the best and most cost-effective way to do so.

Benefits of Part-Time Physicians

The addition of a new, full-time physician to your practice has significant financial ramifications. There will be a need to generate additional revenue as soon as possible to prevent a reduction in compensation for the existing physician providers. One way to minimize this effect is to consider the use of part-time physicians.

Many practices that want to add an additional physician don't immediately need a full-time physician. Usually the growth in demand is such that a part-time person can handle the additional load at first. If this is the case, consider hiring a part-time physician. Depending on your local market, there may be opportunities to hire physicians who want to work only a few days a week. If so, this can be a cost-effective way to solve your needs.

Before making the decision to go with a part-time physician, you will need to check into the limitations this may create and other financial considerations such as the availability of medical malpractice insurance for part-timers.

Paying for an Additional Physician

The cost of hiring the new physician can be significant in terms of the cash commitment your practice must make. In addition to the actual hiring expenses, there may be a shortfall in revenue for a period of time. Volume of new patient visits for the physician usually grows slowly, as will the revenue from those visits and services. If you have guaranteed a minimum or base salary for the new physician, there may be a negative cash flow for a period of time.

Alternate or additional sources of revenue should be explored. For example, you may wish to consider providing services as a medical director for various entities such as nursing homes, public health or other clinics, or local emergency medical services (EMS) departments. Either you or the new physician may provide services in these areas. You may also consider adding services such as house calls or calls to nursing homes or assisted living facilities (ALFs). This alternative source of revenue is applicable for physician extenders as well.

Under certain circumstances, a local hospital may assist in providing funds for recruitment or salary guarantees. Recent law changes have limited these opportunities, but it is still worth contacting the administrators at the hospitals for which you provide care. They may also have opportunities for paid medical director positions, which can help offset the cost of a new physician.

Containing Costs in Recruitment

Once the decision to hire a physician or physician extender has been made, the process of recruitment must begin. There are several ways to approach recruitment. You must determine which method is the best for your practice and then attempt to contain the costs involved in the process.

Professional Recruiters

There are many professional recruiters available to help in the process of recruiting and hiring a new physician or physician extender. While the fees quoted may seem high, hiring a professional recruiter still may be the least expensive route to take. To determine the true cost, you must look at the services provided by the recruiting firms and what the value is to your practice.

First, you should consider the services of several recruiting firms before determining which one you will use. You should carefully review the services they will provide and the fees they will charge. Only after this process is complete will you be able to determine the best choice. In determining the firms to contact you may wish to inquire with the professional societies or organizations of which you are a member to see if they endorse one or more recruiting firms. You may also ask other physicians in your area if they have used the services of recruitment firms. Once you have made a list, contact each firm and ask for a list of their services and the fees they charge.

Most firms will provide resumes of potential physicians or extenders who meet your requirements. The firms may also arrange for the candidate to visit your practice. In addition, the firms may assist the candidate with others services, such as gathering information about your area or town that will be needed for him or her to determine whether he or she is interested in your practice opportunity. The recruiter may also assist you with employment information or documents and other services that are necessary.

Many recruiting firms have established lists of interested physicians or physician extenders who are actively looking for new positions. As a result, recruiting firms may be able to fill your position very quickly. In addition, some recruiters do a good job of screening potential candidates. This will eliminate unqualified candidates or those who would not be a match for your practice, greatly reducing the time you might spend on interviewing.

Some recruiting firms even "guarantee" hires to the extent that if the new hire does not work out within a specified period of time they will recruit a replacement at no additional cost.

However, there are recruitment firms in business that do not provide many of these services or those that have a poor track record in assisting practices but still charge high fees. Therefore, you must carefully qualify the firms you are considering by asking other clients they have served or check with the endorsing societies for their recommendations and insight. Carefully ask questions of the firms' representatives and get all promises in writing.

Recruiting by Yourself

If you choose to recruit a new physician or physician extender yourself, there are a number of areas of potential cost containment you can consider. Before you begin to recruit, you will need to assess your needs and the opportunities available in your area.

After you have determined the qualifications you want in a new physician or physician extender, you must determine the best method to begin the recruitment. You will first need to generate a list of potential candidates. How you do this is a product of the availability of candidates in your area and the method to reach them. Some methods to reach potential candidates are more expensive than others.

Advertising   Advertising for candidates is a good method to generate a list of potential associates, but advertising costs can be great. One of the most expensive ways to advertise is usually by placing an ad in a large-circulation newspaper. Depending on your area, this may or may not be effective. If you are in a large metropolitan area with a good supply of the type of provider you are looking for, this may work well. But you should also consider other places to advertise.

Specialty newspapers, such as local medical business newspapers, provide a more targeted approach and cost far less per potential contact. Newsletters, which list classified opportunities for the providers you are searching for, can also be effective and cost far less. Check with you professional societies at the local, state, and national level to see whether they provide these services. (See the following sidebar for sources of physician extenders.)

Sources of PAs, NPs, and Midwives

Following is a list of sources of physician extenders that may be helpful in your search for PAs and NPs, as well as midwives.

The MHA Group
Phone: 800 876-0500
Web site: www.mhagroup.com

American College of Nurse Midwives
Phone: 240 485-1800
Web site: www.midwife.org

Midwife Alliance of North America
Phone: 888 923-6262
Web site: www.mana.org

American Academy of Physician Assistants
Phone: 703 836-2272
Web site: www.aapa.org

American Academy of Nurse Practitioners
Phone: 512 442-4262
Web site: www.aanp.org

When placing an advertisement, be sure to list the important requirements you may have for the position so that you can screen unqualified candidates, saving you unnecessary time and money.

Other Methods of Finding Candidates   There are other ways to find candidates to fill your new position that are cost-effective and may save you time. Start by letting the local hospitals know that you are looking for a new associate. Most hospitals receive letters of inquiry from physicians hoping to move to that area. This can be a ready supply of recruits.

You should also talk with the local medical society executives and let them know you are looking. They also receive letters from physicians interested in the area. In addition, they may know of local physicians who are interested in merging their practice with others.

Consider talking with your medical school or residency program as well as any other medical teaching program in your geographic area for potential physicians. These programs not only will know who is available but can give you accurate information as to the physicians' skills and competence. This can be your best source of qualified candidates.

If you are looking for a physician extender, contact the various state societies for the extenders and find out whether they publish a newsletter or operate a job-find service for their members. These, too, can be a cost-effective means of finding candidates who are qualified and licensed in your state.

Once you have found candidates to consider, it is time to begin the process of qualifying the candidates and interviewing the most promising. You will have to do most of the screening services provided by the recruiting firms in the process of finding the right associate, so be methodical and careful and utilize the right help in the search. Doing it yourself can be a big cost-saver and can find the right person for your practice.

Retaining Your Practitioners

The cost of retaining your physicians and physician extenders is far less than the cost of hiring new staff. Make sure you have policies and practices in place that will help retain these individuals, starting with fair and well-thought-out employment agreements, followed by reasonable compensation packages. In addition, make sure you provide the opportunity for effective communication between the professionals in your practice and growth and educational opportunities.

If you address these needs, you will be able to better retain the key providers in your practice and, in the long run, contain the cost associated with professional recruitment and retention.

Chapter 7

Optimal Organization Structures

How physicians choose to organize and operate their practices can have a significant effect on cost containment. While the preceding chapters in this book have dealt with specific areas of operation that can impact a practice's costs, the structure within which the practice functions has not yet been discussed.

This chapter looks at a number of ways a practice can be structured to help contain costs. The analysis of the various alternatives is therefore limited to their effect on *cost*—no attempt will be made to analyze other effects of such structures that may have significant impact on the practice and physicians. Before considering any change in a practice's structure, all potential effects must be reviewed and analyzed. For example, in *Practice Affiliation: Forming or Joining a Partnership or Group Practice*,[1] Barbara Hoagland indicates that physicians consider both philosophical and practical considerations when choosing the structure of their practices. Often the philosophical considerations outweigh the practical in the decision-making process. Because these philosophical issues can affect so much of the decision, they should be given careful attention.

Changes in the practice of medicine brought on by managed care have also created an impact on the organizational structure of the physician practice. The demand for greater information on the amount and quality of care has put pressure on the cost side of the equation. Making the decision to participate or not participate in a health plan requires the ability to gather data on your practice's costs. Deciding to offer new services or add new diagnostic tests and procedures, again, requires the data for proper analysis. The right organization can help provide this information in a cost-effective way.

The ability to operate a practice in a cost-effective manner is greatly determined by the availability of qualified individuals and effectiveness with which they are used. It is necessary to keep the number of employees to a minimum because of the cost in retaining them. At the same time, this seems counter to the need to have enough qualified help. How you meet these needs will have an effect on how you organize your practice.

The optimal organizational structure, therefore, is a combination of the acceptable philosophy and the most efficient organization.

Solo versus Group Practice

The decision to practice in a group setting or on your own has many considerations.

It is clear that the number of physicians choosing to practice in a solo setting is declining. Between 1991 and 1995 the number of physicians in solo practice declined by 22%, from a total of 34.1% in 1991 to 26.5% in 1995.[2] At least part of the reason for this trend is the need for physicians to practice more efficiently. Studies have shown that large groups are more efficient than solo practices.[3] Such efficiency is determined not only by practice costs but also by physician productivity.

Staff Costs

Demands on practices to provide more data to third-party payors along with increased administrative duties have put pressure on practices to add more administrative personnel. In addition to quantity, the quality of staff required has been elevated. Dealing with complex regulations for billing and managed care operational requirements have forced practices to hire a higher level of employee.

The cost of staff has been a big factor in the lower efficiency of solo practices. The ability to share new staff with multiple physicians does not exist. Hiring part-time staff with specific skills such as managed care billing and collections is more difficult than hiring full-time staff. In addition, it is cost-prohibitive to hire qualified practice managers in a solo practice.

Conversely, group practices are able to hire specialists in various areas of practice operation because of the practice's larger revenue base. And the cost of a well-trained practice manager is within the financial ability of a larger group practice.

Well-trained and experienced practice managers, whether they are called office managers, practice administrators, or chief operating officers, can have a significant impact on practice costs. The implementation of the various strategies listed in this book requires an individual with good training and understanding in the operations of a medical practice. Such an individual is compensated at a higher level than are most general office workers. However, such a person should be able to save the practice an amount far in excess of his or her salary and benefit costs. Still, it is hard to justify such a highly paid position in a solo practice. Clearly, staff costs can be held to a more reasonable level in a group practice and become more reasonable as the group increases in size.

The number of clinical staff necessary to run the practice generally increases in the same proportion as physician providers, so there tends not to be a cost benefit in this area as the number of providers grows.

Forming a Group Practice

There are two ways to approach the formation of a group practice. If you are currently in a solo practice, you can recruit new physicians to join your practice, thus forming a group. The alternative is to merge your solo practice into an existing group practice. While the two methods require different legal steps and documents, the end result is the same.

Before you form or join a group, it is important to clearly define the reasons you have for taking this step. Those reasons can help identify your goals and give you the basis for a business plan necessary to achieve success. In addition, if one of your purposes in forming or joining a group practice is to help reduce or contain costs, you should make a list of the areas in which you hope to achieve the cost savings.

Once you have identified the areas of potential cost savings, you must carefully analyze each to determine how you plan to reduce costs. Too often practices think they will realize savings before they restructure, only to find out later that the changes actually led to increased costs.

Personnel Questions

As one of the greatest areas of cost for a practice is in personnel, staffing is the logical place to start an analysis. Generally it is wise to divide the personnel into *clinical* and *administrative* to begin this analysis.

Questions to be asked and answered include:

- Can you share staff with an additional practitioner?

- Which staff will have to be added to the new group practice?

- Can existing staff be let go?

Be realistic in your analysis and include your practice administrator in the process. Also, remember to add the other costs of personnel into your calculations, such as employee taxes and benefits.

General Overhead

Another area to analyze is the effect on general overhead in the formation of the group. Will more office space be needed? How much new equipment will have to be purchased? What will the effect be on utilities and insurance? Carefully make these calculations.

Variable Costs

Finally, consider the effect the group formation will have on the variable cost of the practice, such as office supplies, medical supplies, and other supplies. It is also important to factor in any potential savings you may receive by being able to order larger quantities of these supplies.

Sharing Office Overhead

Another alternative to forming a group practice or adding a practitioner to your practice is an arrangement to share office overhead with an independent physician. Such arrangements provide many of the cost savings of adding practitioners but with limited responsibility and organization dynamics.

Under this type of an arrangement, a practice will provide a workplace for an independent physician and provide some or all of the support services needed for an agreed-upon fee. Such arrangements can reduce the practice's overhead expenses for each physician and still enable independence of the physicians.

A carefully worded agreement, which specifically lists the services provided and the expectations of the parties to the agreement, is critical. And, as with any affiliation, a careful evaluation of the physician who will share the space must be undertaken to make sure the practice styles are compatible.

Understanding the Effect of Economies of Scale

It is common to hear that by getting bigger you will benefit from economies of scale. Basically this statement means that you will use less resources to produce a greater volume of goods or services. This maxim works in some cases but not in all cases.

Don't assume that bigger is always more cost-effective. You must first understand the nature of expenses and how they are affected by volume of services to determine whether an increase in service volume will realize cost benefits. In *Medical Practice Accounting & Finance: A Practical Guide for Physicians, Dentists, and Other Medical Practitioners*, Rose Marie Bukics and Donald Chambers explain the different characteristics of fixed, variable, and semivariable costs[4]:

Costs that are *fixed* for a given practice will not change with an increase in volume and therefore can be considered to be contributory to an economy of scale. Such costs as rent and depreciation don't change with an increase of patients or the addition of a new practitioner, assuming you have adequate space in the office and don't buy new, expensive equipment. However, if it is necessary to move the office to allow for more space, a new fixed cost must be calculated.

Costs that vary in direct proportion with the volume of services provided are referred to as *variable costs*. Good examples of variable costs in a practice are medical supplies and office forms. If the volume of patients increases by 20%, these costs will also go up by 20%. As a result, variable costs will not be a factor in calculating any economies of scale. It is important to remember that, should the volume of some of these expenses increase, such as supplies, it may be possible to reduce your per-unit cost by receiving a volume discount in purchasing.

Many costs fall under the category of *semivariable* or *step variable*. These types of costs will remain fixed for a range of volume increase or decrease and then increase to a higher fixed level over the next range of volume increase or decrease. Personnel costs generally fall under this classification of costs. A practice may be able to see five or six more patients during a day without the need to hire more staff. But at some point the volume increase will require that you hire a new staff member. At that point the cost jumps up to a new level for personnel costs. Your ability to calculate the points at which these types of costs will increase is important to calculating the potential of obtaining cost efficiencies as your practice increases volume.

Additional Methods to Contain Costs Organizationally

In an effort to optimize the organizational structure of a practice, several other options exist that can lead to cost containment. These options are generally referred to as *outside affiliation options*.

Solo practices that do not want to consider expansion into group practices or groups that do not want to expand may wish to consider the following options to help meet the demands of the current medical marketplace without expanding their office overhead significantly. As was discussed earlier, one of the most significant areas of cost pressure is in the area of personnel costs. Practices are seeing the need to provide more sophisticated billing and practice management systems, the need to hire seasoned practice managers, and the need to deal with more and more complicated regulations, while the pressure to reduce or contain costs is the greatest it has ever been. Rather than trying to meet these demands internally within the practice, several options exist that can address these needs at a lower cost.

Practices can affiliate with outside organizations that provide many of the services needed without the up-front investment. One such type of affiliation is with a management services organization (MSO). In *Integrating the Practice of Medicine: A Decision Maker's Guide to Organizing and Managing Physician Services*, Paul DeMuro defines an MSO as "an organization that provides services to physicians and physician group as well as others."[5]

MSOs have increased in number in the past few years. Many were started as a result of failed physician practice management companies. As practices were purchased and run by these practice management companies, the individual practices lost the ability to provide certain services within the practice. When the companies failed and either sold or gave back the practices to the physicians, the practices were not equipped to perform the tasks. Companies were formed that were able to provide these services, and in many cases, these companies could do so at a lower cost than the individual practices could.

Some of the services provided by MSOs include billing and collections, group purchasing, managed care contracting services, utilization management, and management information services. Because of their size, many MSOs are able to contract for greater discounts in supplies and other services used by the physician practices. The MSOs are also able to keep up with changes in regulations and billing requirements more easily. In addition, some of the challenges of personnel administration are eliminated for the physicians.

As with all alternatives that may lead to cost savings, the services and costs involved with the affiliation with an MSO must be carefully reviewed. A cost analysis of the services provided and the cost to the practice must be undertaken to determine whether you are truly saving money under this alternative. It is also important to check references for the MSO to see if the practices they provide services to are happy with the arrangement.

Other affiliations such as with independent practice associations (IPAs) and physician hospital organizations (PHOs) may provide additional alternatives. Such affiliations will probably provide fewer services than an MSO but will likely cost less too. Areas of strength for IPAs and PHOs generally lie in the areas of managed care plan operations and control and information systems. In some cases the IPAs or PHOs may contract with an outside MSO to provide some or all of these services.

As with the MSO, you must carefully evaluate the IPA or PHO before you consider affiliation. Some widely discussed failures of these organizations have reinforced the necessity to approach such a decision with care and good information. Still, there are good and effective IPAs and PHOs in business, and they do offer an alternative to providing in-house services in some areas.

However you choose to organize your practice, remember that there are potential cost savings to be realized with the right alternatives. Carefully evaluate these options and develop the optimal organization structure for your practice.

Endnotes

1. Hoagland B. *Practice Affiliation: Forming or Joining a Partnership or Group Practice.* Chicago, IL: American Medical Association; 1990.

2. *Socioeconomic Monitoring System Survey, 1991-1995.* Chicago, IL: American Medical Association.

3. Emmons DW, Kletke P. Physician practice size, 1991-1995. In: Connors RB, ed. *Integrating the Practice of Medicine: A Decision Maker's Guide to Organizing and Managing Physician Services.* American Hospital Publishing; 1997.

4. Bukics RM, Chambers DR. *Medical Practice Accounting & Finance: A Practical Guide for Physicians, Dentists, and Other Medical Practitioners.* New York, NY: Probus Publishing; 1995.

5. DeMuro PR. Evolution of management services organizations. In: Connors RB, ed. *Integrating the Practice of Medicine: A Decision Maker's Guide to Organizing and Managing Physician Services.* American Hospital Publishing; 1997.

Chapter 8

Patient Satisfaction: How am I Doing?

When Ed Koch was Mayor of New York City he frequently asked his constituents a simple yet apparently effective and efficient question of "How am I doing?" In a nutshell, this is what we are doing when we attempt to gauge patient satisfaction.

Unfortunately, many of the medical practices we are familiar with do little to nothing in the patient satisfaction area. However, customer or consumer satisfaction surveying is obvious in other aspects of life, namely, restaurants, automobiles, electronics and with many other consumer products. In order for medical office practices to prosper and to profit, it is our contention that collecting and utilizing patient satisfaction is both worthwhile and increasingly essential for success in today's health care environment.

Google Search

A Google search which linked "patient satisfaction and private practice" resulted in 985,000 pages of literature. A review of these articles found that many of the references oftentimes merely mentioned patient satisfaction in the write-up. Nevertheless, the Google search illustrated that patient satisfaction is acknowledged as a vibrant care management tool in various health care settings such as radiology, oncology, mental health, family practice, physiotherapy, psychiatry, psychology, and general practice to name a few.

Elizabeth Woodcock (2005) notes that satisfaction surveys reflect the voice of the customer. Practices should use surveys to ensure that their operation is meeting the needs of the patients and referring physicians (pg. 134). Christopher Guadagnino (2003) states that the measurement of patient satisfaction stands poised to play an increasingly important role in the growing push toward accountability among health care providers (pg.1).

Marie Reed, Kelly Devers and Bruce Landon (2003) believe that patient satisfaction surveys, which provide an important measure of quality in health care from the patient's perspective, have achieved widespread acceptance by physicians (pg.5-6). D. Andrew Loblaw, Andrea Bezjak and Terry Bunston (1999) state that "Patient satisfaction is an important patient-centered outcome to measure, is accepted as a standard measure of quality of care, and is steadily gaining in popularity" (p.1937).

The *Yale Practice* (1999) newsletter informed its readers that "Reviewing your practice's patient satisfaction survey results" were one of its top 10 tips for a healthy practice (p.3).

To further illustrate the importance of patient satisfaction surveys, Laura Landro (2005) recently wrote in the *Wall Street Journal* about the Centers for Medicare and Medicaid Services launch of the first national survey of patients' perceptions of hospital care possibly as soon as June, 2005. The 27 item questionnaire will cover issues ranging from how well doctors and nurses plan treatments and control pain, to whether patient rooms were clean and patients got help with bed pans or going to the bathroom (p.D1).

Although many hospitals will participate in the voluntary survey there are already some criticisms. Landro (2005) mentions that Christy Stephenson, CEO, Robert Wood Johnson University Hospital in Hamilton, New Jersey, feels that questions about bed pans are absurd and Stephenson doesn't believe these type of questions will measure quality (p. D1).

Assessing Patient Satisfaction

There are numerous ways to measure patient satisfaction. A Google search for "Measuring Healthcare Patient Satisfaction" resulted in 20 pages of citations numbering about 120,000 pages.

Physicians in medical practice should begin slowly, but they need to begin this process of surveying patient satisfaction. Medical practices can either outsource this task to a consultant (vendor) or to a professor in academia who is engaged in this work. Medical practices can also perform this task internally, but usually will need some sort of outside assistance. This last approach allows the practice more control and if properly conducted could be more cost effective.

For a good article on this topic, medical practice personnel can read Meryl D. Luallin (2004), Sullivan/Luallin Inc., San Diego, California, who published "Implementing Patient Satisfaction Survey Findings into a Customer Service Action Plan." In this article, Luallin writes about many of the essential points for implementing patient satisfaction surveys in a simple, lucid format.

The National Committee for Quality Assurance (NCQA) compiles a list of "certified vendors" (vendors who are qualified to collect Health Plan Employer Data and Information Set (HEDIS) survey results. Their list is available at http://www.ncqa.org.

Some of the experts or outside consultant vendors are as follows:

Press Ganey Associates
404 Columbia Place
South Bend, Indiana 46601
Phone: 800-232-8032
Fax: 574-232-3485
http://www.pressganey.com

NCR + Picker, a division of National Research Corporation
1245 Q Street
Lincoln, Nebraska 68508
Phone: 800-388-4264
Fax: 402-475-9061
http://www.ncrpicker.com

The Myers Group
2351 Henry Clower Boulevard
Snellville, Georgia 30078-3107
Phone: 770-978-3173, ext. 302
Fax: 770-978-6267
http://themyersgroup.net

Information can also be obtained on patient satisfaction surveys from the following:

American Academy of Family Physicians
11400 Tomahawk Creek Parkway
Leawood, Kansas 66211-2672
Phone: 800-944-0000
http://www.aafp.org

American Medical Group Association
1422 Duke Street
Alexandria, VA 22314-3430
Phone: 703-838-0033
Fax: 703-548-1890
http://www.amga.org

Medical Group Management Association (MGMA)
P.O. Box 17603
Denver, CO 80217-0603
Phone: 877-275-6462
http://www.mgma.com

Rand Corporation
P.O. Box 2138
Santa Monica, California 90407-2138
Phone: 310-393-0411
http://www.rand.org

Many academic universities have graduate and undergraduate students who could be utilized in patient satisfaction surveys. Some academic disciplines that might prove helpful include Health Administration, Program Evaluation in Social Work, Psychology, and various departments in Schools of Business, Public Health, Nursing and Education, respectively. Oftentimes, faculty can enlist responsible students as a part of an internship to help coordinate, collect and analyze the data.

The third approach is for physicians to obtain previously utilized questionnaires and use as is or modify them to get the patient satisfaction process started. Many times networking and professional organizations can assist medical practice in discovering what is available and how to obtain and implement it. Medical offices could also obtain copyrighted and/or standardized questionnaires from some of the identified experts or vendors.

An excellent example of one such measurement device is the American Academy of Family Physicians (AAFP) "AAFP Patient Satisfaction Survey" from its Vital Signs: Taking the Pulse of Your Practice project. The booklet by Michael Gordon and Susan Rehm (1996) discusses the rationale and importance for conducting patient satisfaction surveys and it includes 6 appendices with samples. The AAFP survey is a 23-item (2 page) survey with one open ended section for a comment. The direct contact person for obtaining more information about the survey is Penny Pine, Practice Enhancement and Senior Program Coordinator, telephone 800-274-2237 (ext. 4148) or e-mail ppine@aafp.org.

For a list of books on Patient Satisfaction see Appendix D.

Tips for Questionnaires

1. **Questionnaires should be "short and sweet."** In most cases strive for 1 to 2 pages.

2. **Questionnaires should be clear.**
   This means ask questions that patients will know what you are asking. No medical mystification.

3. **Questionnaires should cover the primary areas of patient satisfaction.**
   From our literature review this means that quality issues (satisfaction with medical care), access issues (ease in making appointment or obtaining a referral) and interpersonal issues (physicians and staff caring and compassionate) must be addressed.

4. **Completed questionnaires should be rewarded.**
   Patient's time is valuable too. Patients who complete questionnaires should receive some remuneration. For short questionnaires, perhaps $2 to $5 per survey and/or a drawing for a prize(s).

5. **Questionnaires should have stamped self addressed envelops if mailed.**
   Make it as easy as possible for patients to complete and return.

6. Questionnaires need to be analyzed.

After the information is collected it is important to analyze the data in a timely fashion.

7. Questionnaires results should be fedback and used for changes if indicated.

In addition to being used to benchmark the medical practice, changes might be indicated from the survey and they should be acknowledged and implemented whenever feasible.

Sample Survey

Some examples of patient satisfaction surveys follow. Philip O. Alderson, MD (2003) cites a sample regarding a 15-item list patient satisfaction instrument used in radiology.

Figure 8.1: Sample of a patient satisfaction survey

This postcard is mailed to patients shortly after their visit. On one side of postcard are survey questions; on the other side (not shown), the address of the practice conducting the survey and return postage are provided. (Courtesy of E.J. DeSalvo, MD, Strategic Outpatient Services)

A Google search discovered a 2001 seminar entitled, "Using Patient Satisfaction Data to Provide Feedback and Improve Clinic Performance," by James E. Davis, M.D., M.S. and Les Moffet, M.B.A., University of Wisconsin Medical School, Department of Family Medicine. The authors present a 15-item questionnaire developed by MD Powell and A. Kristen entitled, "UW Health Family Physicians Patient Satisfaction Survey."

Julie Sanderson-Austin (2005) stated that the original 9-item medical outcome study patient satisfaction survey was developed by Ronald Hays at Rand Corporation. The original survey was modified with permission by the American Medical Group Association to include 4 additional questions. (The University of Wisconsin Medical School added 2 questions.)

Figure 8.2: UW Health Family Physicians Patient Satisfaction Survey

POWELL MD, KRISTEN A

UWHealth

Family Physicians

Patient Satisfaction Survey

Thinking about your visit with the person you saw, how would you rate the following: (Fill one bubble per line.)

	Poor	Fair	Good	Very Good	Excellent
1. How long you waited to get an appointment	O	O	O	O	O
2. Convenience of the location of the office	O	O	O	O	O
3. Getting through to the office by phone	O	O	O	O	O
4. Length of time waiting at the office	O	O	O	O	O
5. The personal manner (courtesy, respect, sensitivity, friendliness) of the office staff	O	O	O	O	O
6. Time spent with the person you saw	O	O	O	O	O
7. Explanation of what was done for you	O	O	O	O	O
8. Technical skills (thoroughness, carefulness, competence) of person you saw	O	O	O	O	O
9. The personal manner (courtesy, respect, sensitivity, friendliness) of the person you saw:	O	O	O	O	O
10. The visit overall	O	O	O	O	O
11. In general, would you say your health is	O	O	O	O	O

	Definitely not	Probably not	Probably yes	Definitely yes
12. Would you recommend the person you saw to your family and friends?	O	O	O	O
13. Would you recommend the medical care at this clinic to your family and friends?	O	O	O	O

	Male	Female
14. Are you (patient) male or female?	O	O

15. How old are you (patient)? [ ][ ][ ] Years   Example: [7][2] Years

Office use only

O Scheduled   O Walk-in

Payer Code
O CAID   O OTR
O CARE   O SP
O HMO/PPO   O MC
O INS

FormCode   ClinicCode SiteCode   Doc Id
0978023569   8001   11   64184

Rand (1994) had a 16 page survey entitled, *The Patient's View on Health Care* and the subsection "Your Health Care" covers questions 10 through 16 as follows.

Your Health Care

The questions below refer to the health services you have received from your medical group. Thinking about the place you go for your regular health care (that is, your medical group), how do you rate the items listed below? For each question, please grade the care you receive from Very Poor (F) to The Best (A+) by circling one number on each line. If something does not apply to you, mark "Does Not Apply to Me."

10. How do you rate . . .   **(Mark One Number on Each Line)**

	Very Poor (F)	Poor (D)	Fair (C)	Good (B)	Very Good (B+)	Excellent (A)	The Best (A+)	Does Not Apply to Me
a. Convenience of the location where you get care	1	2	3	4	5	6	7	0
b. Quality of treatment you receive	1	2	3	4	5	6	7	0
c. Medical staff listening to what you say	1	2	3	4	5	6	7	0
d. Arrangements for parking	1	2	3	4	5	6	7	0
e. Answers to your questions	1	2	3	4	5	6	7	0
f. Medical staff's effort to make visit comfortable and pleasant	1	2	3	4	5	6	7	0
g. Hours that the place you get care is open	1	2	3	4	5	6	7	0
h. Ease of getting prescriptions refilled	1	2	3	4	5	6	7	0
i. Quality of examinations you receive	1	2	3	4	5	6	7	0
j. Ease of reaching the medical staff by phone when you have problems	1	2	3	4	5	6	7	0
k. Ease of speaking with your primary care provider by phone	1	2	3	4	5	6	7	0
l. Thoroughness and accuracy of diagnoses	1	2	3	4	5	6	7	0
m. Friendliness and courtesy shown to you by the receptionist and other front desk staff	1	2	3	4	5	6	7	0
n. Ease of seeing the primary care provider of your choice	1	2	3	4	5	6	7	0
o. Explanations about prescribed medicines	1	2	3	4	5	6	7	0

	Very Poor (F)	Poor (D)	Fair (C)	Good (B)	Very Good (B+)	Excellent (A)	The Best (A+)	Does Not Apply to Me
p. Access to a specialist when needed	1	2	3	4	5	6	7	0
q. Explanations of medical procedures and test results	1	2	3	4	5	6	7	0
r. How long you wait in the reception area	1	2	3	4	5	6	7	0
s. Amount of time spent waiting in the exam room before seeing your primary care provider	1	2	3	4	5	6	7	0
t. Friendliness and courtesy shown to you by your primary care provider	1	2	3	4	5	6	7	0
u. Ease of getting hospital care when needed	1	2	3	4	5	6	7	0
v. Advice you get about ways to avoid illness and stay healthy	1	2	3	4	5	6	7	0
w. Ease of getting medical care in an emergency	1	2	3	4	5	6	7	0
x. Friendliness and courtesy shown to you by nurses and other medical staff	1	2	3	4	5	6	7	0

11. For each of the following, could the health care you now receive be: improved a lot, some, not much, or is no improvement needed?　　**(Mark One Number on Each Line)**

	A Lot of Improvement Needed	Some Improvement Needed	Not Much Improvement Needed	No Improvement Needed	Does Not Apply to Me
a. Ability to choose your primary care provider	1	2	3	4	0
b. Ability to obtain the treatment you need	1	2	3	4	0
c. Communication between the medical staff (doctors, nurses, etc.) who treat you	1	2	3	4	0
d. Availability of services tailored to your needs	1	2	3	4	0
e. Reminders or encouragement to use timely preventative services (such as blood pressure checks, mammograms, etc.)	1	2	3	4	0
f. Amount of time you wait for health care services to be approved	1	2	3	4	0

g. Amount of time you wait
   before being able to get an
   appointment with a specialist
   when you need one 1   2   3   4 | 0

12. How do you rate . . .   **(Mark One Number on Each Line)**

	Very Poor (F)	Poor (D)	Fair (C)	Good (B)	Very Good (B+)	Excellent (A)	The Best (A+)	Does Not Apply to Me
a. Reassurance and support offered to you by doctors and staff	1	2	3	4	5	6	7	0
b. Ease of scheduling appointments by phone	1	2	3	4	5	6	7	0
c. How well your primary care provider informs you about the costs of care	1	2	3	4	5	6	7	0
d. Amount of time you must wait between scheduling an appointment for routine care and the day of your visit	1	2	3	4	5	6	7	0
e. Number of primary care providers you have to choose from	1	2	3	4	5	6	7	0
f. Amount of time you have with doctors and staff during your visits	1	2	3	4	5	6	7	0
g. Training, skill and experience of the nursing staff	1	2	3	4	5	6	7	0
h. Your primary care provider's concern for your mental health or emotional well-being	1	2	3	4	5	6	7	0
i. Availability of educational materials or programs to enhance your health	1	2	3	4	5	6	7	0
j. Comprehensiveness of routine checkups and physicians	1	2	3	4	5	6	7	0
k. Ease of getting lab and radiology work completed when ordered by your primary care provider	1	2	3	4	5	6	7	0
l. Ease of getting a referral to a medical specialist	1	2	3	4	5	6	7	0
m. Ease of getting a referral to a mental health specialist . .	1	2	3	4	5	6	7	0
n. The office environment (cleanliness, comfort, lighting, temperature) where you get care . .	1	2	3	4	5	6	7	0

o. How well your care meets
   your needs 1   2   3   4   5   6   7   0
p. Overall quality of care and
   service provided by your
   medical group 1   2   3   4   5   6   7   0

13. **During the last 6 months,** how many times *in total* did you use your medical group's
    "after hours or urgent care services"?   **(Mark One)**

    Not at all 1
    1 time...2
    2 times..3
    3 to 5 times 4
    5 or more times 5

14. Do you plan to switch to a different medical group when you next have an opportunity?
                                                              (Mark One)

    Definitely yes 1
    Probably yes...2
    Probably not...3
    Definitely not 4

15. What is the name of your health plan (e.g., Health Net, CIGNA, etc.)?

    _____

16. How long have you been enrolled in your current health plan?
                                                              (Mark One)

    Less than one year 1
    1 to 2 years...2
    3 to 5 years...3
    More than 5 years......................................4

Conclusion

We believe that the benefit of establishing, implementing and continuing surveys of patient satisfaction not only empower patients, but it also empowers medical practices. Using this care management tool can lead to improved patient loyalty and referrals as well as help practices gain market share. Patient satisfaction surveys can also help identify, measure, and monitor aspects of medical practice that are primary determinants of patient satisfaction.

Patient satisfaction surveys continue to gain popularity and medical practices need to be progressive and proactive in implementing them on a regular basis. Medical practices need to know how they are doing so that they might be able to provide the best possible care. The customer (or patient) really is king or queen and he or she pays our bills. Recognition of this is not only respectful, but is sound business practice.

References

Alderson, Philip O. Customer Service and Satisfaction in Radiology, "*American Journal of Roentgenology*," 2000, 175, 319–323.

Davis, James E. and Moffett, Les. "Using Patient Satisfaction Data to Provide Feedback and Improve Clinic Performance," STFM 2001 Seminar.

Gordon, Michael and Rehm, Susan. *Patient Satisfaction Surveys*. Kansas City, MO: American Academy of Family Physicians, 1996.

Guadagnino, C. "Role of Patient Satisfaction," *Physician's News Digest*. December 2003.

Landro, Laura. "How did You Find Our Jell-O? Government Prods Hospitals to Survey Patients on Quality: Gauging the Bathroom Factor," *Wall Street Journal*, April 20, 1995, D1.

Loblaw, D. Andrew, Bezjak, Andrea and Bunston, Terry. "Development and Testing of a Visit-Specific Patient Satisfaction Questionnaire: The Princess Margaret Hospital Satisfaction with Doctor Questionnaire," *Journal of Clinical Oncology*, 1999, 17, 1931–1938.

Luallin, Meryl D. "Implementing Patient Satisfaction Survey Findings into a Customer Service Action Plan," *Journal of Medical Practice Management*, 2004, 20, 90-94.

Reed, Marie C., Devers, Kelly and Landon, Bruce. "Physicians and Care Management: More Acceptance than You Think." Center for Studying Health System Changes Issue Brief no. 60, January 2003.

Telephone interview with Penny Pine, American Academy of Family Physicians, May 6, 2005.

Telephone interview with Julie Sanderson-Austin, American Medical Group Association, June 6, 2005.

Woodcock, Elizabeth W. "Practice Benchmarking" (Chapter 11) in Wolper, Lawrence F. *Physician Practice Management: Essential Operational and Financial Knowledge*, 2005, Jones and Bartlett.

Yale Practice Newsletter. http://info.med.yale.edu/yfp. January 1999.

Chapter 9

Technology's Role in Cost Containment

Too often when new technology is considered for medical practices it is seen as an additional cost to be borne. There is usually a debate between the benefits of such technology, usually its improvement to quality outcomes, versus the additional cost the practice must incur if it decides to go forward with the new application. Part of this problem is created by the developers and manufacturers of the technology. For too long the health care industry has developed various pieces of equipment, new procedures and new types of support technology with but one guiding principle: to improve the quality of care through better diagnosis, treatment and outcomes. If the new technology or equipment costs more, we have justified it only by the outcomes it produces and we have accepted the increasing cost as a necessary factor in its use.

It appears that the health care industry is the only major industry in the country that will produce and utilize new equipment or technology without consideration for its cost effect on the product it sells: health care. Most industrial equipment is designed, manufactured and sold with the justification that the new equipment will not only produce a better product, sometimes at a faster rate, but also at a reduction in cost per output unit. Few if any industrial companies would buy a new, expensive, piece of equipment or other type of technology if they could not justify the capital outlay with a reduction in overall cost per item produced.

Healthcare, on the contrary, has sought to produce better methods to diagnosis and treat patients through the introduction of newer and improved equipment, procedures and technology with no driving concern for the cost of such new methods. It could be argued that the method of paying for health care has created this mind set as the payers of health care have not always been concerned with the cost of an individual treatment but only the overall costs of care which they have been able to pass on to their customers, whether employers who purchase health care for their employees or directly to individuals who purchase their own insurance.

That is not to say that advances in equipment, treatment and medical technology have not indeed produced better results and lowered cost at the same time. We have just not looked at cost cutting with as critical a role as we should have nor felt pushed to do so. Those times have changed.

The pressure to reduce costs in health care is particularly focused on the individual medical practice as it sees reimbursement declining through contractual agreements with third party payers and recent pressure to reduce charges to self paying patients. And, as reimbursement declines the cost of providing the necessary care seems to continue to rise.

As a result it is time to look at how a practice can use new technology to reduce its costs and to accurately determine which types of technology and equipment can produce the desired results of lowering costs.

There are brief discussions throughout the book that look at certain types of technology and their effect on cost containment. This chapter will look at several types of new technology and show how technology may help a practice further contain the cost of running the practice. Electronic Medical Records (EMR), E-mail, Websites and other clinical and administrative applications will be reviewed to help identify their role in cost containment in the medical practice.

Electronic Medical Records (EMR)

The benefits of an electronic patient record are well documented in the literature. Patient safety is touted as one of the first and most advantageous uses of an EMR, not only in a physician's office but in other health care settings such as hospitals, clinics and even for regional health care consortiums. The positive effect on work flow in a medical office as well as the ease of reviewing patient records is a huge benefit of the EMR. The ability to share patient information with more than one individual at the same time can only be efficiently accomplished with some type of electronic records storage. But, when faced with the cost projections of implementing such a system in the doctor's office, EMR vendors are turned away quickly. How can an office add yet another cost to the practice and still stay in business?

Interestingly, when practices that have fully implemented an EMR have been asked about the cost of the system and how long it has taken to pay for it, you will hear time frames of from two years to less than one year. How can this be?

Properly designed and implemented EMR's will indeed reduce the costs of a practice. If you have not considered one, maybe now is the time to look more deeply into it.

Cost components of an EMR

When getting a cost estimate for an electronic medical record system, there will usually be four components to be considered. There will be the cost of the software, which you must license from the developer or vendor, the cost of the hardware needed to run the software, the ongoing cost of updating the hardware and software and the cost of maintaining the system. Sometimes it is not clear from the proposals you obtain from vendors as to how much these individual costs will be.

Software: An EMR system is driven by the software that was developed to capture the patient information and to make it available to the users of that information. In most cases this will be the single largest component of the initial cost of the EMR system. You can typically purchase a license for the software or enter into an agreement to utilize the software on an ASP (Application Service Provider) model over the internet.

The selection of the software is a time consuming process as there are literally hundreds of companies producing EMR software currently. While this chapter is not designed to discuss the process of selecting EMR software or hardware it must be said that the process is critical to the potential cost savings to be had from such a system. If a particular EMR does not provide the ability to accomplish cost cutting functions or is not easily implementable then you will not accomplish the desired savings.

Hardware: As with all software applications, you must have the appropriate hardware to make it run. Some EMR software can be run on existing hardware in some offices particularly if the office has considerable other software applications in use such as practice management systems, automated diagnostic equipment and other computer assisted functions. If you feel you have the necessary equipment in house it is important to check with the EMR software vendor to verify the hardware's compatibility with their software. Typically, though, a practice will need to purchase new or additional hardware to effectively utilize the EMR system software and components. To analyze the cost of the hardware you should check with the chosen software vendor to develop a complete list of hardware components that you can shop with. Usually the software vendor will offer to sell you the hardware but you can also purchase it from traditional hardware vendors. You should check both sources to establish the most cost effective place to purchase the hardware.

Cost of updating the software and hardware: As with all technology driven solutions or applications, there can be a significant cost to updating the software and hardware. As improvements are made in the software, as new governmental requirements require changes to the software and as you choose to improve specific functions within your EMR system, there is a cost to you. Most EMR software vendors or developers have a staff of programmers dedicated to improving the general operation of the software and to make necessary changes to comply with governmental regulators and the ever changing regulations imposed on the health care industry. Most EMR vendors/developers offer this service on an ongoing basis through new updated versions of the software and most will charge a set yearly price for this service. Make sure you factor this cost into you analysis of the cost of the EMR system. Estimating the cost of custom changes to your EMR system is more difficult to determine. At a minimum, find out the cost your EMR vendor/developer will charge for these custom changes and attempt to include a reasonable amount of these services in your software maintenance contract. And as the complexity of the software increases, you may find it necessary to update of purchase new hardware to take advantage of the changes. While this will not happen as frequently as the software is updated, you should attempt to project any hardware updates or additions that can be reasonable anticipated. Hardware that may be necessary to start using new components of the software that you chose not to purchase initially is a good example of anticipated hardware purchases.

Cost of maintaining the system: The ongoing cost of maintaining the EMR system will primarily be related to the maintenance of the hardware. A maintenance contract can usually accomplish this task at a predetermined price. However, if the system you are installing is of considerable size based on the number of users and the amount and complexity of the hardware needed to run the system, you may need to hire technology personnel to maintain your system. In determining this need it is essential to talk to the practices of similar sizes that are utilizing the EMR system you are thinking of choosing. They will provide a better source of unbiased information than the EMR vendor/developer. Don't forget to include this component in your cost analysis of the EMR system.

Cost Savings of an EMR

There are several areas where an EMR can generate cost savings and ultimately not only pay for the systems but produce an overall reduction in the practice's overhead. Some or all of them may apply to your practice.

Medical Transcription: For practices with significant transcription needs, the proper EMR can reduce or eliminate this expense. Typically practices with large consultative services or specialists that must document procedures done pay a great deal for transcription services. Many EMR's provide the necessary features to automate the transcription process and produce appropriate written reports without the necessity of paying for a transcriptionist. Through the use of standard templates or the use of voice recognition software, an individual practitioner can produce their own reports with speed and accuracy. Before assuming that the EMR you are considering can do this, be sure to verify the type and method used to produce reports and determine their accuracy and suitability to your style of practice. In many cases the cost savings from transcription services will pay for the new EMR by itself. This is an area worth exploring.

Medical Records Staff: In large practices a staff of medical records personal handle all aspects of the patients' records from creating the basic record to filing reports and lab results as well as coping and sending records to third parties. An EMR can greatly reduce the number of hours needed for these tasks in addition to providing quick access to the patients' records to practioners in the office. In most cases, multiple staff members can access a single patient's record at the same time and no one will spend the afternoon looking for the patient's chart in the office. An honest evaluation of the cost savings in this area can go a long way to paying for an EMR system.

Office supplies: How much can a few pieces of paper and a folder cost? That is a good question to ask your office administrator. The supplies to create and maintain a patient record can be significant. To the actual patient's record costs you should add the other office supplies that go to creating and maintaining a patient record like extra paper for notes and diagnostic exam reports down to pencils and pens. You may be surprised how much is spent on the creation and maintenance of a chart.

Records storage: Another significant area of potential cost savings from an EMR, the costs associated with the storage of records, can be greater than you think. Most practices find themselves buying additional patient storage shelves as their practices grow and many rent storage facilities to keep older records off site. Most if not all of these costs will go away in the short term. Electronic storage is relatively cheap and is, if done properly, more safe than storage of a physical medical record.

Other areas of savings to consider: As you think about the functions your EMR does you will start to find other areas of savings, particularly in staff salaries. With enhanced coding assistance in most EMR's you will be able to cut the cost of coders and billers in your practice. Occasional costs of couriers and persons to go to the records storage facility to retrieve records will go away. With careful analysis of the EMR you are considering and a good look at the work flow in your office, the areas of cost savings are many.

There have been considerable discussions recently among medical organizations and malpractice insurance companies about the possibility of offering premium discounts on medical malpractice policies for providers utilizing EMR's. This may be yet another area of cost savings in the near future.

When making the decision to purchase an EMR system the question of paying for the system is important. You have the option to purchase out right, lease or utilize an ASP model. The question of lease versus purchase is dealt with in another chapter (Chapter 4) in the book and should be reviewed to help with the decision process.

Integrated versus stand alone systems

EMR's typically fall into three categories. There are EMR's that are fully integrated with other practice software such as a practice management system, there are EMR's that are stand alone systems that are not designed to share information with other practice software, and there are EMR's that are developed by companies that only design EMR's but are able to be linked to and share data with other practice software systems.

If part of your decision process is your concern for the cost savings an EMR system can provide for your practice, you need to be careful to evaluate which of these three types of EMR's you are buying. Clearly, the most efficient and therefore the best potential for cost savings lie with fully integrated systems. Because the various components of these systems are designed within the same company they usually have little technical problems sharing data between the component programs or functions. That is to say, when basic patient demographic information is entered into a computer in the system, that information is automatically available to all components in the system. There is no need to re-enter that data to be used in a different part of the system. Likewise, when clinical information is entered into the EMR component of the system, that data is also shared with the other components of the system such as the billing module of the system.

A negative to buying a fully integrated system is the overall cost of the system. Remember, you are buying both an EMR software program and the hardware needed to utilize it and you are buying a practice management or other software system and the hardware to utilize them too. If you currently have a practice management system that is meeting the needs of your operations and are interested in adding an EMR, check to see if the same company offers a fully integrated EMR module. Of course, you must research that EMR system to see if it is functional and effective for your practice. The purchase of an EMR from the same vendor as your practice management system, that does not work well in your practice setting is not a wise purchase, just because it is integrated.

Because most practices have an existing practice management system, and because there are not a large number of vendors of practice management system that offer fully integrated EMRs, most practices that are considering adding an EMR look at companies that develop only EMR's. In many cases, these companies have spent considerable time developing their software and their EMRs tend to be very feature oriented, especially in one or more medical specialty areas. These systems are designed to meet the complete needs of a clinical EMR and usually start in one clinical area and then expand to others as the company grows.

With all EMRs it is important to be sure the system will work effectively with your particular specialty. As the needs of medical record documentation vary by specialty, most EMR developers work on particular specialties, one at a time. The effort is spent making sure the various templates and links between patient data are appropriate for the needs of the practitioners in that specialty. Simply stated, an EMR designed to be effective for an otolaryngology practice probably does not offer the tools needed for a cardiology practice. Smaller EMR developers do not usually have modules specific to all medical specialties and are therefore not able to provide systems for all practices. Most of the larger developers have spent time and money developing EMR modules for large numbers of specialties and can therefore market to a larger target market. Make sure a system you are considering meets your practices needs.

Most EMR developers claim their systems will integrate to most practice management systems. This is a claim that must be researched. There have been many cases where EMRs were installed and linked to a practice management system only to find that they do not fully share data between the systems are don't share the data at all without expensive custom software development not originally anticipated. If you have found a good EMR for your practice and are considering buying it you should not only check with other EMR users but you should check with your practice management software company to see if they can give you names of practices that have effectively linked that EMR to their system. Don't take the word of the vendor's sales staff. Seek out and question practices that are actually using, or trying to use both systems.

The uses of EMRs that do not link with practice management software in an office are not typically significant cost savings producers. These "stand alone" systems are used in unique practice situations in specialty areas not targeted by EMR companies on a large scale. While they may be good tools for a practice these systems rarely result in cost savings.

Compatibility considerations between EMR systems

As more and more health care organizations, including physician practices, implement EMR or EHRs (Electronic Health Records) and develop area wide or regional networks, referred to as RHIOs, to capture and share patient health information among many groups and people, the need to use systems that can be compatible with other systems becomes an issue to consider. While larger systems capturing and sharing patient information will lead to even more cost savings for physician practices, more time and research will be necessary to pick appropriate systems.

Before making a final decision you should check with any hospitals you may be on the staffs of to see what their plans are for implementing EMRs. Also check with other physician organizations you may be a member of or are considering joining to see if they have plans for implementing EMR's or being part of a RHIO. A number of physician organization, such as IPAs, PHOs and medical societies, have recently started to become involved in EMR technology. In some cases, they may be a source of capital funding for an individual physician's practice EMR and may even offer ongoing customer support for an EMR. Additionally, even if the hospital or physician group will not help with an individual practice's EMR, you may want to be sure you EMR will be fully compatible with their proposed systems.

E-Mail as a Cost Savings

Virtually everyone uses E-mail to communicate in some way. Even the senior population is embracing E-mail and the internet. Yet, most practices have not yet begun to use E-mail to communicate with their patients. In addition to being a more effective method of communicating with patients than the telephone it is an area of potential cost savings. Probably this biggest area of cost savings will be the reduction of phone line expenses and the potential to reduce staff. In addition to cost savings, it may also have a significant effect of patient satisfaction.

Staff time spent on answering phone calls and making return calls is a significant cost in most practices. When evaluating practice operations most say that they spend too much time on the phone and the calls interrupt the office routine and reduce efficiency of staff. That is because when a phone rings, someone must answer it at the time it rings. More often than not, the caller either has a question for a staff member who cannot come to the phone at that time or they need information that the staff member answering the call does not have at their finger tips. As a result, at least one call back will be required for each incoming call and many times more than one will be required. When a call back is not done in a timely manner, the originally caller may choose to call again, thus increasing the number of calls related to a single request to result in 3 or more total calls. Staff time is significant.

Developing a system to utilize E-mail for your patients who are comfortable with this mode of communications can help solve this problem. By developing a very clear E-mail policy that patients must agree to, the time spent communicating by phone can be reduced as well as the staff time needed. In a busy practice, it is possible to eliminate multiple phone lines and replace them with a single DSL or other broad band access method. It may also be possible to reduce staff.

The office E-mail policy should establish what types of communication will be allowed using E-mail, how long the office will take to respond to any E-mail and the security and privacy requirement the practice has regarding the use of E-mail. The more you can do via E-mail the more time and money you can save. Of course privacy issues are important and you must develop a system that meets both the HIPAA privacy and security rules. There are several physician organizations that offer help with such policies that are worth researching. The AMA has developed "Guidelines for physician-patient electronic communications" which is available at their website www.ama-assn.org/ama/pub/category/2386.html. You may also check with Medem, Inc., which is an organization created by the AMA and a number of medical specialty societies to assist with communications efforts between physicians and patients. Their suggested guidelines can be found at www.medem.com/phy/phy_eriskguidelines.cfm.

Regarding establishing a time frame for E-mail responses, it is important to be very clear to the patient when you will respond to their request. For instance, you might establish a policy that says you will respond to all E-mails within 12 or 24 hours of their being sent, except for weekends and holidays. You might say that E-mails received by noon each day will be responded to by 5:00 PM that day or E-mails received after noon will be responded to by noon the next day. By setting an expectation with the patient, you will reduce the number of repeat e-mails/communications with the patients and by giving you staff enough time to research the patient's question; you will reduce the number of multiple calls needed to answer the patient's questions. And, by using E-mail, you will never get an answering machine that you cannot leave a message on and breach the patient's privacy. Remember, you must address privacy and security in your E-mail policy and should get the patient to sign the policy and place it in their file (or scan it into their EMR).

Websites Role in Cost Containment

Well designed websites for physician practices can also offer cost savings benefits due to more cost effective approaches to operations. Many physicians see websites as marketing or education tools only. But, with proper planning and design a website can be used to communicate with patients more effectively, allow patients to make their own office appointments and renew prescriptions with less staff involvement. The educational component of a website can translate into cost savings by reducing staff time with patients to provide needed patient education as well as reduce medical malpractice risk by more effectively providing informed consent via well designed explanation of procedures and tests requiring patient consent. These presentations can be developed by or for your practice exclusively or are available from third parties that will license their use or allow free use. Checking with medical malpractice company's risk management operations will provide a wealth of information on available products you can add to your website.

Remember, that if you are communicating private health information over your website, you must make sure the proper encryption software is being used. For that reason it is highly advisable to utilize a web development company that has significant experience in health care web site development. You may also want to check with your local medical societies, state societies or other physician organizations to see if they can recommend website developers who will offer you discounts on the development costs. Remember we are trying to cut costs. Don't, however, select a low cost developer that can not deliver a high quality site that protects patient privacy and help you save practice expenses.

Other potential savings from the use of technology

Development of new technology solutions to physician practice problems are continuing at a rapid pace. Some will offer improved clinical outcomes such as disease management software. These clinical programs have the potential not to improve patient care and outcomes but to provide your practice with a new source of revenue. Pay for performance programs being developing and being used by managed care companies rely heavily on being able to document improvements in patient outcomes or adherence to established treatment protocols. Technology provides the tools to not only help a practiced follow these protocols but to document the outcomes.

Most existing programs are stand alone software but these functions are being added to more sophisticated EMR programs and will eventually be a standard feature in most EMR's on the market. If you contract with managed care companies, check to see if they are offering or planning to offer pay for performance programs. If so, it will be just one more reason to look more carefully at adding technology to your practice.

Other uses of technology in medical practices which will either cut costs or increase revenues are being developed at a rapid pace. Some technology currently exists that can produce these benefits but will probably wait until the payers of health care, either directly by patients or from third parties, realize the value and begin to provide reimbursement for such services. The potential for telemedicine to provide added, inexpensive health care services to patients using technology is only waiting for payment for such services to become accepted and available. In addition, as with most advances in medical technology, we will wait for the legal barriers to be lowered so that we can take advantage of new services that can be provided more efficiently and more effectively. For example, physicians providing care or consultation to patients in underserved areas in other states without the specter of being guilty of practicing medicine without a license if the patient resides in a different state different from the doctors license(s).

A final work of caution

While technology offers the opportunity of significant savings for a physician's practice, there is a need for a well organized and well researched due diligence function in the decision process to purchase and implement the technology. Claims of costs and potential revenue made by vendors of the technology cannot be taken at face value. You or your representative must check out each claim and validate each and every critical point in the decision making process that effects the potential value and cost savings you are counting on from the technology.

The decision on how you finance this technology can also make a significant difference in the ultimate outcome of you decisions.

Probably, the most important component in the decision making process you will go through in your decision to buy and implement new technology will be the assessment of you and your practices commitment to the successful use of the technology. There are many, well designed EMR systems that offer real cost savings and tools to provide better clinical care that are purchased by practices and are sitting unused because there was not the commitment from the physician(s) and/or the office staff leadership to make sure it would work in their practice. In those cases a potential cost saver has become a cost producer.

Chapter 10

Cost Savings Through Affiliated Organizations

T he volume of services and products purchased by most physicians and their practices are relatively low even for the larger groups. As a result, obtaining "quantity discounts" is not typical for most physicians. However, when physicians come together through formal organizations, the quantities of goods and services used by the total membership of the organizations maybe high enough to negotiate quantity discounts.

Most physicians and practices belong to a number of organizations related to their practice of medicine. These organizations may be professional in nature or they may be some type of a "trade" organization. Most if not all of these organizations have realized that because of the number of members or participants, they have some clout in negotiating for products or services for their members. A careful review of the various programs and organizations can yield a significant number of programs that can save your practice money on various routine costs associated with your practice.

Physician Organizations

Most organizations you belong to were not created for the purpose of obtaining cost savings on the purchases you make in your practice. But, many of the organizations you belong to have negotiated discounts for products and services that you, as a member, can take advantage of. Let's look at some of the organizations physicians might belong to.

Professional Organizations: Organizations that have been established to recognize, regulate and support physicians as professionals will fall into this category. At the top of the list is the American Medical Association, probably the largest professional organization for physicians. While some may see the AMA as a trade association, it probably is truly a professional organization. Next on most physicians' list of professional organizations will be their national specialty professional organization. Typically this will be the organization that confers board certification in a particular specialty. Many doctors hold membership and board certification in more than one of these organizations.

Regionally, there are also professional organizations, usually organized around specialties. They may be a single state or in some cases multiple adjacent state organizations. Included in this list would be state medical societies and county medical societies.

The larger the professional organization the greater the ability to negotiate discounts for products and services.

Trade or other non-professional physician organizations: There are numerous such physician organizations in existence and the chances that any one physician is a member of at least one is quite high. Included in this list would be organizations such as IPAs (Independent Physician Association), PHOs (Physician Hospital Organizations) MSOs (Management Services Organizations) and special interest organizations. While none of these organizations were started with the intent to obtain discounts on products and services, most have realized that they have the ability to do so and have therefore done some negotiating on behalf of their members.

Searching for the discounts

Most physician organizations that have successfully negotiated discounts for products and services for their members advertise them. Check regular publications, such as newsletters, magazines and E-letters they send out. You should also check the websites of the organizations to look for a link to member discounts. You can also call the office of the organization and ask if they have such a program. You may have to search as some of these organizations do not do a great job of promoting these benefits. If a particular organization does not offer any discount programs, you should suggest they consider doing so and make a formal request to their operating officers or board of directors for them to initiate such programs.

Types of discounts available

The more popular discount programs offered by physician organizations include supply and equipment discounts. Again, while the amount of supplies used by the typical physician practice is not necessarily high, a group of several hundred physicians can represent enough volume to negotiate good discounts for the individual members. Office supplies as well as clinical supplies are prime targets for negotiating discounts. It is important, however, to check the prices carefully to see is the discounted prices are truly better than you currently get and to see if there is any volume guarantee you must meet in order to receive these discounts. Discount prices for supplies can sometimes be difficult to evaluate as the vendor may not give an across the board percentage discount off the posted price. If the discounts are enumerated by an actual price list of all items being discounted, you will need to match your practice's supply purchases and prices with those on the discount list from the vendor. In many cases you may find that some items are cheaper and some are more expensive. If this occurs you will need to consider the volume of each item to see if the net effect is a true savings to you.

Some negotiated discount programs offer supplies or equipment of a similar type to what you currently use but not an exact product match. In these cases, you must evaluate the quality and usability of the alternate, less expensive products to see if you can or want to use them in your practice.

If you have chosen to use the discount programs it will be necessary to price shop from time to time. Depending on the actual agreement with the physician organization with the vendor, prices may go up unannounced. To protect from paying too much, your office manager (or other staff who is responsible for ordering supplies) must do a periodic comparison with other vendors to assure you are still getting the best prices.

It will also be necessary to check carefully with discount programs for equipment. While the equipment prices may be lower that other companies or programs you must check to see if you are obligated to purchase associated supplies used by the equipment as a term of the contract to receive the discount on the original equipment. If you must purchase supplies used by the equipment vendor, compare their prices with other vendors of the needed supplies and check to see if the prices offered by the equipment vendor can be locked in for a reasonable period of time. Usually a reasonable lock in period is from one year to the length of the useful life of the equipment being purchased.

Outside billing and collecting services are another area where physician organizations negotiate discounted rates. These highly competitive businesses are very interested in negotiating the percentages or fees they receive for their services if they can be assured of a larger base of clients. As with all discount programs, it is important to analyze the quality of the service being offered by the contracted vendor of these services. A few percentage points off a collection service that does not collect as efficiently as another at a slightly higher price is a net loss to your practice. Evaluate each company as you would any other vendor by asking for confirmation of their performance in writing and talk with other physicians' practices that are currently using them.

Technology is another big area of potential discounts available from physician organizations. For similar reasons as other suppliers, technology vendors would like to sell a greater number of their products to as many physicians as they can. Therefore, they are interested in negotiating discounts with these physician organizations so they can market to the individual physician and offer the incentive of a discount off their regular pricing. But, with technology, there are other benefits possible for the individual physician by buying through such an arrangement. One of the important components in a successful technology solution system is the availability of technical support. Some very well written software programs are not supported particularly well due to a low volume of customers (physicians) or a relatively small presence in a geographic area. While some of the technical support for technology can be effectively supplied over the internet or the telephone, other aspects such as training of new personnel require face to face support.

If a physician organization negotiates a good discount on a type of technology needed by its members and the number of members who buy that technology is high enough, it is also possible to negotiate local technical support from that technology vendor. In other cases the physician organization can offer the support to its members who purchase the systems.

Another product/service that has seen significant success in physician organization contracting is medical malpractice insurance and risk management programs. While not a new undertaking by physician organizations, the recent pressure on reasonably priced and available medical malpractice insurance has pushed physician organization contracting into the forefront. Both professional physician organizations such as specialty societies as well as trade organizations such as IPAs and PHOs have ventured into this area with good success. In many cases these organizations have been able to put together programs which have generated discounts of 5–10 percent or more which translates into thousands of dollars of savings per year for members.

To be successful, these programs must be carefully designed with the help of medical malpractice insurers or other experts in the medical malpractice arena. They must be legally permissible by the state or areas in which members will participate and they must be financially sound for the insurers.

By establishing high underwriting criteria for participants, a lower risk group of doctors can be identified and marketed to medical malpractice insurers in the market. Once established, the physician organization or subset of that organization working with the insured physicians must aggressively monitor claims and provide ongoing risk management programs to both the insurer and the physician members to keep the discounted premiums in effect.

Such malpractice programs are not usually all inclusive of a particular physician organization membership. That is, not all members of a physician organization may qualify for these programs due to underwriting criteria.

Other types of coverage arrangement for medical liability can also be developed by physician organizations such as insurance off shore captives and domestic captives as stand alone or as cells of a larger group. Entering into these arrangements takes a great deal of research and a significant amount of expertise and management to be successful. With that said, they are still worth a look as the cost savings can be significant for the physician.

The list of discounted items that can be negotiated by physician organizations is endless. The basis behind these types of cost savings programs is the use of large numbers needed to negotiate lower prices for goods and services. Take the time to see what discounts are offered by physician organizations you are a member of and whether they are of real value to you is cutting your costs.

Afterword

Managing a medical practice can be an arduous task if the physician is not properly organized. The key to successfully operating a medical practice efficiently and cost-effectively is twofold: First, the physician must have a carefully thought-out plan to approach the task. Second, the physician must understand the concepts and methodologies that have been presented in this text and must be willing to utilize these tools in making changes.

It is common for a physician to read a text such as this and decide that his or her practice could benefit from making changes that will aid in managing costs. Unfortunately, many physicians begin the process but fail to bring it to fruition because the process entails some steps that require extra work or skill sets that he or she does not possess, or creates a potentially unpleasant situation for a short period of time.

Physicians desiring to modify practice operations to enhance cost savings and improve efficiency must commit to working through the necessary processes. Once the changes have been planned, implemented, and monitored, the practice will begin to experience positive improvements. Many of these improved operational efficiencies will occur gradually and a reduction in costs will be noted over time.

It is important to remember that in analyzing the results of the changes made to the practice that the physician look at trends over a period of time from 3 to 6 months. Reviewing changes on a weekly or monthly basis will not allow for peaks and valleys in performance. Therefore, it is important to study trends over an extended time period and fine-tune the various parts of the practice as needed.

The practice that sees the benefit in improving operations, analyzes the practice's needs, properly plans changes to be made, and utilizes an implementation plan will be successful in attaining its goals. Remember, an efficiently and effectively managed practice will have many of the following benefits:

- The practice will more readily adapt to industry changes in the future.

- Expenses will decrease and workflow will be more efficient.

- The practice stress level will decrease and the staff will be happier and more productive.

The ability to operate an efficient and cost-effective practice rests solely with the physician. If you are willing to make the commitment, you will reap the benefit.

Leading Health Care
IT Companies

Following is a listing of the top 25 health care system vendors in the marketplace today, as ranked in the June 2005 issue of *Healthcare Informatics*.

Rank		Company Name and Location	Primary Business
2005	**2004**		
1	—	Cardinal Health Dublin, Ohio (800) 234-5000 www.cardinal.com	Develops, manufactures, packages and markets products for patient care; develops drug delivery technologies; distributes pharmaceuticals and medical, surgical and laboratory supplies; offers consulting and other services that improve quality and efficiency.
2	2	Philips Medical System Andover, Mass. (800) 722-7900 www.medical.philips.com	Provides patient monitoring and ultrasound systems, information management, medical IT, diagnostic cardiology devices, resuscitation products, Xray, MR and CT, nuclear medicine and PET-related supplies, professional services and support.
3	—	Agfa–Healthcare Business Group Ridgefield Park, N.J. (877) 777-2432 www.agfa.com/healthcare/us	With global experience in imaging and IT, connectivity, technical and professional services, healthcare business consulting and clinical applications, Agfa is committed to being a trusted total healthcare management partner.
4	3	EDS Plano, Texas (760) 599-4171 www.eds.com	A knowledgeable and experienced IT services firm, with a strong team of 6,000 global healthcare professionals standing ready to tackle your challenges.
5	5	McKesson Provider Technologies Alpharetta, Ga. (404) 338-6000 www.infosolutions.mckesson.com	Provider of IT solutions that help organizations worldwide to improve patient safety, reduce the cost and variability of care, and better manage revenue stream and resources.
6	6	ACS Inc. Dallas (214) 841-6000 www.acs-inc.com	Provider of fully diversified, end-to-end, business process outsourcing (BPO) and IT solutions to commercial and government clients worldwide; comprehensive solutions delivered to all segments of BPO and IT services.

Rank		Company Name and Location	Primary Business
2005	**2004**		
7	7	WebMD Corp. Elmwood Park, N.J. (201) 703-3400 www.webmd.com	Provides products and services for physicians, consumers, providers and health plans that streamline administrative and clinical processes, promote efficiency and reduce costs by facilitating information exchange, communication and electronic transactions.
8	8	Computer Sciences Corp. El Segundo, Calif. (610) 251-0660 www.CSC.com	Globally organized to serve providers, payers, pharmaceutical, medical device and biotech clients as well as federal, state and national healthcare agencies through management consulting, systems integration and outsourcing agreements.
9	9	Cerner Corp. Kansas City, Mo. (816) 201-0000 www.cerner.com	Supplier of healthcare IT, taking the paper chart out of healthcare and eliminating error, variance and waste in the care process.
10	10	Perot Systems Corp. Plano, Texas (888) 317-3768 www.perotsystems.com	Leverages deep expertise in consulting, business processes, applications, and IT infrastructure to craft integrated, industry-specific solutions that support business strategies and facilitate improvements for its customers.
11	—	Dell Inc. Round Rock, Texas (512) 728-4100 www.dell.com	Diversified IT supplier and partner that sells a comprehensive portfolio of products and services directly to customers worldwide.
12	1	GE Healthcare IT Waukesha, Wis. (800) 558-5120 www.gehealthcare.com	GE Healthcare's IT business creates software and IT solutions for healthcare facilities of all sizes, to improve clinical performance; expertise spans clinical information systems and PACS, to enable real-time, integrated EMR.
13	4	Capgemini New York (917) 934-8000 www.capgemini.com	Provides holistic solutions in technology, consulting, and outsourcing; healthcare practice specializes in clinical transformation, process improvement, revenue cycle and supply chain services.
14	11	Ingenix Inc. Eden Prairie, Minn. (888) 445-8745 www.ingenix.com	Global health IT and consulting company offering broad range of solutions to enhance clinical and financial insight, increase quality of healthcare delivery and administration, and manage costs.
15	14	IDX Systems Corp. Burlington, Vt. (888) 439-6584 www.idx.com	Provider of software, services and technologies for healthcare provider organizations.
16	12	Misys Healthcare Systems Raleigh, N.C. (800) 334-8534 www.misyshealthcare.com	Develops and supports reliable, easy-to-use software and services of high quality that enable physicians and caregivers to more easily manage the complexities of healthcare.

Rank		Company Name and Location	Primary Business
2005	2004		
17	13	NDCHealth Atlanta (800) 778-6711 www.ndchealth.com	Offers network and system solutions to automate exchange of information among pharmacies, payers, hospitals and physicians; improves operational efficiencies and business decision making for providers, retail pharmacy and pharmaceutical manufacturers.
18	15	Per-Se Technologies Inc. Alpharetta, Ga. (877) 737-3773 www.per-se.com	Offers connective healthcare solutions that enable physicians and hospitals to achieve income potential by creating environment that streamlines and simplifies the complex administrative burden of providing healthcare.
19	21	Eclipsys Boca Raton, Fla. (561) 322-4321 www.eclipsys.com	Provider of advanced clinical, financial and management information software and service solutions to more than 1,500 healthcare facilities.
20	24	Epic Systems Corp. Madison, Wis. (608) 271-9000 www.epicsystems.com	Supports the enterprise with an integrated clinical, access and revenue cycle system that connects hospitals, clinics, patients and affiliates; delivers optimized workflows and customer service for the entire organization.
21	20	Concentra Inc., Network Services Div. Addison, Texas (800) 232-3500 www.concentra.com	Technology outsourcing and financial services that assist payers in review and administration of medical bills associated with group health, workers' compensation and auto injury claims.
22	17	Medical Information Technology Inc. (MEDITECH) Westwood, Mass. (781) 821-3000 www.meditech.com	Provides integrated software solutions that meet information needs of healthcare organizations worldwide, including hospitals, ambulatory care centers, physicians' offices, long-term care and behavioral health facilities, and home health organizations.
23	—	Science Applications International Corp. Falls Church, Va. (888) 886-5909 www.saic.com/healthcare	SAIC's Health Solutions Business Unit provides clinical information system, life science and research, health data integration and management, public health and cost containment solutions to federal healthcare clients.
24	16	TriZetto Group Inc., The Newport Beach, Calif. (949) 719-2200 www.trizetto.com	Offers comprehensive enterprise software, outsourcing and professional services that help healthcare organizations achieve their business vision, with less risk and improved ROI.
25	18	FCG Long Beach, Calif. (800) 345-0957 www.fcg.com	Provider of outsourcing, consulting, systems implementation and integration for healthcare, pharmaceutical and other life sciences organizations throughout North America, Europe and Asia.

Physician Practice Management System Selection Evaluation

Following is a sample evaluation form to use when selecting a physician practice management system for your practice.

Vendor Script and Evaluation Criteria	Available	Not Available	Excellent (E), Good (G), Satisfactory (S), Unsatisfactory (US), Does Not Apply (DNA)	Comments
Patient Registration				
Enterprise-wide patient number and registration				
Ability to perform registration for another site				
Comprehensive patient registration and editing functionality				
Copy of demographic information from screen, patient guarantor				
System edits for duplicates, etc.				
Adequate space for addresses, information, free text				
Audit trail on registrations and changes				
System information: • HMO/PPO subscriber number • Cash required alert				
User-defined information for insurance coverage screen				

Vendor Script and Evaluation Criteria	Available	Not Available	Excellent (E), Good (G), Satisfactory (S), Unsatisfactory (US), Does Not Apply (DNA)	Comments
Automatic benefits and eligibility check through online links				
Patient chart/charge ticket, labels, user-defined forms				
15+ user-defined patient notes				
Provide for preregistration to capture demo data prior to visit				
Ad hoc reporting graphs				
Provide batch interface to accept registration data from other systems				
Ability to set up and retrieve of HMO/PPO eligibility data				
Registration of recurring/series patient				
Multiple fee schedules				
Ability to time stamp for patient check-in				
Discuss process of online eligibility reporting and review				
Discuss how the membership database works				
Patient surveillance module and statistics reporting				
Discuss system ability to "flag" collection accounts				
Discuss referral tracking				
Discuss patient "look-up" (inquiry)				
Provider Maintenance				
Track provider credentials				
Contract renewal dates and warn of expiring contracts				
Historical tracking and statistics				
Check patient assignments from registration				
Link referral providers to individual or network contracted payment arrangements				
Track hospital affiliations with specific privileges				
Charge Posting				
Detailed and summary service reports				

Vendor Script and Evaluation Criteria	Available	Not Available	Excellent (E), Good (G), Satisfactory (S), Unsatisfactory (US), Does Not Apply (DNA)	Comments
Alerts for duplicate charge posting				
Audit checks within the system (eg, reasonableness check, number, % amount, etc.)				
Ability to look up patient by name or number				
Accommodate fourth-and fifth-digit editing of diagnosis code				
Default diagnosis				
Demonstrate audit trail or charge transactions				
Ability to override information (price, procedure, etc.)				
Support multiple fee structures				
Calculation of contractual terms				
Daily and monthly audit reporting				
Denial explanation fields				
Ability to generate ad hoc reports/graphs				
Ability to post to specific charges				
Billing				
Discuss how payor demographics are established/edited				
Discuss claim data requirements, edit checks				
Electronic billing and reporting				
Automated balance billing to secondary payors				
Contract management system and reports				
Discuss handling of capitated contracts				
Ability to perform centralized and decentralized billings				
User-defined reporting				
Discuss audit trails				
Review billing cycle options				
Ad hoc reports and graphs				

Vendor Script and Evaluation Criteria	Available	Not Available	Excellent (E), Good (G), Satisfactory (S), Unsatisfactory (US), Does Not Apply (DNA)	Comments
Claims Processing/Adjudication				
Use of authorized services is linked to claims and payments and how IBNR (incurred but not reported) is documented as claim is paid on the referral				
Autopayment by diagnosis				
Provide sample of IBNR exposure reporting				
Claims processing/adjudication				
User-defined managed care reporting				
Claims Management				
Automated user-defined claims correspondence				
Online subscriber, eligibility, and benefit verification through online link				
Electronic transmission of claims through ANSI standards				
User-defined unlimited edits with claims management and reporting				
Online claim level notes				
Upload or error correction by carrier				
Electronic transmission of claims through ANSI standards				
Electronic funds transfer				
Ad hoc reports and graphs				
Full transmission history				
Generation of copayments and deductibles				
Referral/Authorization				
Link multiple authorizations for patient				
Tight integration with interaction with claims processing				
Ability to document referral management process				
Ability to document authorization process by payor				
Ability to generate referral authorization report/letter				

Vendor Script and Evaluation Criteria	Available	Not Available	Excellent (E), Good (G), Satisfactory (S), Unsatisfactory (US), Does Not Apply (DNA)	Comments
Ability to track number of visits against number of referrals				
Automatically calculate estimated liability based on contracts/authorized services				
Provide IBNR (incurred but not reported) reports				
Provide estimated versus actual liability reports for closed authorizations				
Generate referral and authorization forms. User-defined?				
Detect duplicate authorizations				
Support online unlimited user-defined notes				
Ad hoc reports and graphs				
User-defined reporting				
Collections				
Collection follow-up system				
Online worklists and reports				
Enterprise-wide collections				
What coding schemes are available for comments				
User-defined setup of comments for letters, bills, statements				
Review statement setup and parameters (financial class, age balance, patient type, practice, groups)				
Autodialing capability				
Payment plans and reporting				
Combining of accounts and audit checks				
Monitoring tools and reports				
User-defined bad debt processing				
Automatic letter follow-up routine? Can they be free text?				
Standard and free text messages				
Free text and standard comments use				
Guarantor versus patient billing				

Vendor Script and Evaluation Criteria	Available	Not Available	Excellent (E), Good (G), Satisfactory (S), Unsatisfactory (US), Does Not Apply (DNA)	Comments
User-defined statements				
Ability to send to outside agency user-defined parameters.				
Ability to perform centralized and decentralized collections				
Collector performance tracking				
Ad hoc reporting and graphic capabilities				
Ability to place statement on hold				
Archiving/Security				
User-defined archiving of accounts				
Review security				
Scheduling System				
Integrated scheduling of physicians, rooms, equipment and other resources				
Ability to review schedule on weekly, daily, and monthly basis				
Capture of referring and primary care physician information				
Capture of visit duration information/tracking information				
Additional unlimited information or comments at scheduling				
Outstanding balances.				
Collector notes/alerts at scheduling				
Cancellation of all or part of physician's schedule with automatic search for new scheduling time slot				
Multiple office/facility scheduling with conflicts				
Ability to double or triple book				
Automatic sequence of appointments by test/procedure				
Ability to schedule more than one resource per time and room				

Vendor Script and Evaluation Criteria	Available	Not Available	Excellent (E), Good (G), Satisfactory (S), Unsatisfactory (US), Does Not Apply (DNA)	Comments
Interface to hospital admissions or scheduling for enterprise scheduling				
Ad hoc reporting				
Allow overbooking and overlaps by specific time periods				
Search by patient, day of week, time of day, duration				
Block out times easily, including recurring slots				
Automatic update of all system on appointments				
Bring daily, weekly appointment list				
Ability to report reason for visit				
Multiple physicians on one screen				
Automatically alerts medical records for chart pull				
Ability to monitor patients from check-in to discharge with statistics				
Schedule physicians for at least 6 months				
Ability to produce ad hoc reports				
Ability to define unlimited schedule definitions				
Medical Records				
Computerized patient record				
Electronic signature				
Ability to define treatment protocols with standard templates by specific type				
Customization of patient charts				
Bar coding chart management				
Laptops, palmtops, or portable laptops for clinical documentation that provide real-time update via radio-frequency (RF)				
Problem lists with staging of illnesses				
Acuity weighting tools				
Ease of tools/flowsheets				
Allergy list available				

Vendor Script and Evaluation Criteria	Available	Not Available	Excellent (E), Good (G), Satisfactory (S), Unsatisfactory (US), Does Not Apply (DNA)	Comments
User-defined/free text progress notes				
Automatic tracking of medication history				
Online formulary by payor				
Ability to print prescriptions				
Drug, food, and allergy interactions				
Laboratory/numerical flowsheet form				
Ability to print images, documents into record				
Ability to interface transcription into electronic chart				
Online user-defined correspondence				
Centralized or decentralized chart management				
Ad hoc reports and graphs				
Patient Services Management				
Entry and tracking of patient service issues				
Integrated correspondence/ word processing				
Patient satisfaction monitoring and reporting				
Support of user-defined parameters for tracking and resolution of issues				
Historical database of issues and related information				
User-defined form letters				
User-defined patient service parameters				
Patient Survey generation and reporting/statistics				
Ad hoc reports and graphs				
Wait time tracking				
Payment Posting				
Electronic remittance				
Review payment/system balancing protocols				
Ability to post by name, ID#, SS#, INS#				
Ability to edit				
Ad hoc reports and graphs				

Vendor Script and Evaluation Criteria	Available	Not Available	Excellent (E), Good (G), Satisfactory (S), Unsatisfactory (US), Does Not Apply (DNA)	Comments
Report Generation				
Review report production capabilities				
Discuss system flexibility				
Ease of Use				
Menu-driven with logical structure plain language				
Window-oriented screen displays				
Error messages in plain English				
Speed				
Time to register a new patient (goal: 1 minute)				
Patient access time (goal: 2 seconds)				
Menu searching time (goal: 2 seconds)				
Hardware and Software				
Review purging and archiving				
Operations Management				
Discuss backup protocol				
Describe daily, weekly, monthly processing				
Review the systems management process				
Discuss the company's application support and education				
Reliability				
Backup performed within the program				
Built-in reindexing				
Files editing available				
Vendor is well established				
Source code in escrow				
Program author(s) available				
Telephone support available				
Modem support available				
Discuss downtime and disaster recovery				
Technical Support				
Discuss hardware configuration				
Discuss devices supported by system				

Vendor Script and Evaluation Criteria	Available	Not Available	Excellent (E), Good (G), Satisfactory (S), Unsatisfactory (US), Does Not Apply (DNA)	Comments
Does system support use of PCs as terminals or network devices?				
Is system compatible with area-wide network?				
Credentials				
Track provider credentials				
Contract renewal dates and expiration warnings				
Historical tracking and statistical data				
Check patient assignments from registration				
Electronically link referral providers to individual or network contracted payment arrangements				
Track hospital affiliations with specific privileges				
A/R				
How payor demographics are established/edited				
Claim data requirements, edit checks				
Electronic billing and reporting				
Automated balance billing to secondary payors				
Contract management system and reports				
Discuss handling of capitated contracts				
Ability to perform centralized and decentralized billings				
User-defined reporting				
Discuss audit trails				
Review billing cycle options				
Ad hoc reports and graphs				
Electronic remittance				

Selected Organizations Certifying Office Professionals

The American Health Information Management Association (AHIMA)

In 1991 the American Medical Record Association (AMRA) changed its name to the American Health Information Management Association (AHIMA). It is responsible for establishing excellence standards in health information management. The Web site, www.ahima.org, is a great resource to learn more about the organization and its activities.

Recently, the AHIMA conducted a benchmarking survey and it found that 39% of its members work in physician group practices, 26% work in hospitals/integrated delivery, 21% are employed in ambulatory care/surgical centers, and 14% are employed in managed care. The AHIMA has a membership of over 40,000 professionals who work throughout the health care industry.

Some of the human resources needed for physician practices include the following:

- **Registered Health Information Administrator (RHIA) (formerly Registered Record Administration)**

  RHIAs are skilled in the collection and analysis of patient data. In a recent membership survey, AHIMA found that more than half of the RHIA respondents were directors, managers, or consultants, with nearly 31% serving as health information directors. Minimum requirement is a bachelor's degree.

- **Registered Health Information Technician (RHIT) (formerly Accredited Record Technician)**

  RHITs are health information technicians who ensure the quality of medical records by verifying their completeness, accuracy, and proper entry into computer systems. RHITs often specialize in coding diagnoses and procedures in patient records for reimbursement and research. In AHIMA's recent membership survey, the majority of RHIT respondents held job titles in either of the following categories: coding/technician or manager/supervisor.

  Minimum requirement is an associate degree from an accredited Health Information Technology (HIT) program.

- **Certified Coding Specialist (CCS)**

  CCSs are professionals skilled in clarifying medical data from patient records, generally in the hospital setting. To perform this task, CCSs must possess experience in the ICD-9-CM coding system and the surgery section within the CPT® medical code coding system.

  Minimum requirements are high school diploma and 3 years' on-the-job coding experience and education.

- **Certified Coding Specialist–Physician-Based (CCS-P)**

  The CCS-P is a coding practitioner with expertise in physician-based settings such as physician offices, group practices, multispecialty clinics, or specialty centers. The coding practitioner reviews patients' records and assigns numeric codes for each diagnosis and procedure. CCS-Ps possess knowledge of the CPT® medical code coding system and familiarity with ICD-9-CM and HCPCS level II coding systems.

  Minimum requirements are a high school diploma and 3 years' coding experience and education.

The AHIMA has a wonderful Web site that has a current list of community colleges and undergraduate degree programs by state. In addition, there is complete information on requirements, seminars, and testing sites for certification, as well as continuing education. www.ahima.org

The Professional Association of Health Care Office Managers (PAHCOM)

PAHCOM was founded in 1988 to provide a support system to the managers of physician office practices. It has over 3000 members. For members of PAHCOM who are actively involved in medical office management, there is a certification process. The following information is obtained from PAHCOM's Web site (www.pahcom.com) or interviews with its staff.

- **Certified Medical Managers (CMMs)**

    To qualify for certification, medical office managers must:

    1. Be actively employed as a health care office manager for a minimum of 3 years.

    2. Successfully complete at least 12 college or university credits. (There is an extensive experience recognition option wherein the educational credit requirement is reduced by one credit hour for every year of experience the candidate has above the 3-year minimum. For example, a candidate with 15 or more years of experience would not need any formal education credits.)

    3. Be recognized as a health care office manager by both peers and employer(s).

    Candidates for the CMM must take a two-part written examination. Part 1 is composed of 160 multiple-choice questions about relevant management knowledge in health care. Some of the covered areas are as follows: billing and collections, coding analysis, communication, conflict management, financial planning, human resources, patient education, practice marketing, practice structure, risk management, third-party reimbursement, and time management.

    Part 2 requires the candidate to provide comprehensive responses to two of three case studies that depict complex problems in managing a health care practice. PAHCOM publishes the *PAHCOM Management Guidebook*, which serves as the main text for development of the certification exam.

    PAHCOM also has a requirement of 24 hours of continuing education units (CEUs) every 2 years. This helps ensure CMMs are current about changes in the health care practice environment.

American Academy of Professional Coders (AAPC)

The mission of the AAPC incorporates the establishment and maintenance of professional, ethical, and educational standards for all parties concerned with procedures in coding medical information. Much of the information here is obtained from interviews with the AAPC and from their Web site, www.aapcnatl.org.

Update: As of July 2005, there were 43,000 members of the AAPC.

An example of a recent job from the Academy Coding Edge April 2005 reads as follows:

> Medical specialty society in Alexandria, VA is currently recruiting for a Coding Specialist. This position serves as the primary contact for coding issues. The preferred candidate will have Certified Professional Coder (CPC) certification with work related experience in a health care environment required. Work experience should include CPT/ICD-9 codes, medical billing & collections, and skills in Microsoft Office programs. Experience with otolaryngology or other surgical specialty coding preferred. To apply, send cover letter (required), resume, and salary expectations to: employment@entnet.org or fax: 703/519/1587. Visit website at www.entnet.org to learn more about us.

Medical Group Management Association — (MGMA) the nation's principal voice for medical group practice

The Medical Group Management Association (MGMA), founded in 1926, is the nation's principal voice for medical group practice. MGMA's 19,500 members manage and lead more than 11,500 organizations in which more than 240,000 physicians practice. www.mgma.com

MGMA serves the spectrum of physician practices from small to large, plus other health care delivery systems such as management service organizations, integrated delivery systems and ambulatory surgery centers.

MGMA leads the profession and assists members through information, education, networking and advocacy. Its core purpose is to improve the effectiveness of medical group practices and the knowledge and skills of the individuals who manage and lead them.

MGMA operates two related organizations that provide certification and research. The American College of Medical Practice Executives (ACMPE) is the standard-setting and certification organization for group practice professionals. The MGMA Center for Research is the research companion to MGMA.

MGMA's related organizations

- **American College of Medical Practice Executives (ACMPE)** is the standard-setting and certification body of MGMA. You can also find financial information here.

- **MGMA Center for Research** is the research and development companion to MGMA. The Center for Research, a 501(c)(3) research foundation, conducts quantitative and qualitative research to advance the art and science of medical group management.

Appendix D

Bibliography on Patient Satisfaction

This list was obtained from Amazon.com's listmania and was authored by Kevin B. Piper, Healthcare Strategist and Consultant.

Applebaum, Robert, Straker, Jane K. and Geron, Scott. *Assessing Satisfaction in Health and Long Term Care: Practical Approaches to Hearing the Voices of Consumers.* New York: Springer Publishing, 2000.

Baird, Kristin. *Customer Service in Health Care: A Grassroots Approach to Creating a Culture of Service Excellence.* San Francisco, CA: Jossey-Bass, 2000.

Baker, Susan Keane. *Managing Patient Expectations: The Art of Finding and Keeping Loyal Patients.* San Francisco, CA: Jossey-Bass, 1998.

Cohen-Mansfield, Jiska, Ejaz, Farida K., and Werner, Perla. *Satisfaction Surveys in Long-Term Care.* New York: Springer Publishing, 1999.

Fitzpatrick. *Measurement of Patient's Satisfaction with Their Care.* London: Royal College of Physicians, 1993.

Fottler, Myron D., Ford, Robert C. and Heaton, Cherrill P. *Achieving Service Excellence: Strategies for Healthcare.* Chicago, IL: Health Administration Press, 2002.

Leebov, Wendy and Scott, Gail. *Service Quality Improvement: The Customer Satisfaction Strategy for Healthcare.* San Francisco, CA: Jossey-Bass, 1993.

Leebov, Wendy, Vergare, Michael, and Scott, Gail. *Patient Satisfaction: A Guide to Practice Enhancement.* Oradell, NJ: Medical Economics Book, 1990.

Leebov, Wendy. *Customer Service in Health Care*. Chicago, IL: American Hospital Publishing, 1990.

MacStravic, R. Scott. *Creating Consumer Loyalty in Healthcare*. Chicago, IL: Health Administration Press, 1999.

Nash, David. *Connecting with the New Healthcare Consumer: Defining Your Strategy*. Sudbury, MA: Jones and Bartlett, 2001.

Nelson, Anne-Marie, Wood, Steven D., Brown, Stephen W., Bronkesh, Sheryl and Gerberg, Zachary. *Improving Patient Satisfaction Now: How to Earn Patient and Payer Loyalty*. Sudbury, MA: Jones and Bartlett, 1997.

O'Malley, John F. *Ultimate Patient Satisfaction: Designer, Implementing, or Rejuvenating an Effective Patient Satisfaction and Tqm Program*. New York: McGraw-Hill, 1992.

Press, Irwin. *Patient Satisfaction: Defining, Measuring, and Improving the Experience of Care*. Chicago, IL: Health Administration Press, 2002.

Saxton, James W. and Leaman, Thomas L. *Managed Care Success: Reducing Risk While Increasing Patient Satisfaction*. Sudbury, MA: Jones and Bartlett Publishers, 1998.

Schneider, Carl E. *The Practice of Autonomy: Patients, Doctors, and Medical Decisions*. New York: Oxford University Press, 1998.

Shelton, Patrick. *Measuring and Improving Patient Satisfaction*. Sudbury, MA: Jones and Bartlett, 2000.

Sherman, Stephanie G., Sherman, Clayton V. *Total Customer Satisfaction: A Comprehensive Approach for Health Care Providers*. San Francisco, CA: Jossey-Bass, 1999.

Sommers, Paul A. *Consumer Satisfaction in Medical Practice*. New York: Haworth Press, 1999.

Warner, K.C., Zhand, Mark and Wilson, Mary. *Patient Centered Care: Your Prescription for Maximum Patient Satisfaction and Loyalty*. Charlotte, NC: Warner Development, 1996.

Index

Physician hospital organizations
  (PHOs), 83–84, 112, 115
Physician organizations, 111–115
  professional, 111–112
  searching for discounts offered by,
    112–113
  trade or other non-professional, 112
  types of discounts offered by,
    113–115
Physician practice(s)
  assessing patient satisfaction with,
    85–96
  benchmarking of, 5–7
  creation of multispecialty practice,
    68
  electronic systems of, 15–19
  manual systems of, 10–15
  multiple sites of, 47
  office layout of, 14–15
  organizational structures for, 77–84
  physician extenders in, 68–70
  process improvement for, 9, 11,
    22–23
  re-engineering of, 9–11
  reviewing systems of, 9–27 (*See also*
    Office systems)
  successful operation of, 117–118
  websites for, 14, 107
PLA (preventive legal audit), 65
Powell, M. D., 91
Practice expenses. *See* Expenses
Practice flow, 11, 13–14
Practice management information
  systems, 17–19
  demonstration of, 18
  determining needs for, 17
  electronic medical records systems
    linked with, 102–104
  form for evaluation of, 123–132
  selection of, 17–19
  vendors of, 18, 119–121
Practice managers, 78–79, 135
Press Ganey Associates, 87
Preventive legal audit (PLA), 65
Privacy, of Internet communications,
  106, 107

Process improvement, 9, 11, 22–23
Productivity, 10–11, 13
Professional Association of Health Care
    Office Managers (PAHCOM),
    135
Professional organizations, 111–112
Professional recruiters, 72–73
Property management, 46–47
Pulakos, Elaine, 38
Purchase decisions, 54–55. *See also*
    Lease/purchase decisions; Leases
  factors involved in, 55
  for office space, 46–47
  sales tax consequences of, 55
  for technology, 108
Purchasing cooperatives, 43–44

Q

Quality of care, 21t, 86

R

Rand Corporation, 88
Re-engineering, 9–11
Real estate taxes, 49
Records storage, 102
Recruitment of employees, 29–39, 42
  conducting interviews for, 36–39
  employment application for, 30–35
  of "good" employees, 29–30
  job descriptions for, 30
  methods of, 30
  reference and background checks for,
    30, 35–37
Recruitment of practitioners, 67–75
  adding physicians, 70–71
  advertising for, 73–74
  benefits of part-time physicians,
    70–71
  containing costs in, 72–75
  decision to add staff, 68
  determining need for additional staff,
    67
  finding appropriate candidates for,
    73–75

hiring physician extenders, 68–70
paying for additional physicians, 71
screening candidates, 72
using professional recruiters for,
72–73
Reed, Marie, 86
Reference checks
for consultants, 59
for employees, 30, 35–36
Referrals
patient, 11
for personnel recruitment, 30
Regional health information
organizations (RHIOs), 104–105
Registered health information
administrator (RHIA), 133
Registered health information
technician (RHIT), 134
Rehm, Susan, 89
Rented office space, 47–50. *See also*
Leases
Request for information (RFI), 17, 43,
53
Request for proposal (RFP), 17, 26, 43,
53
Retention of practitioners, 75
Revenue sources, 71
RFI (request for information), 17, 43, 53
RFP (request for proposal), 17, 26, 43,
53
RHIA (registered health information
administrator), 133
RHIOs (regional health information
organizations), 104–105
RHIT (registered health information
technician), 134
Risk management systems, 115
Roediger, Joan M., 5
Rokeach, Milton, 30
Russell, Joyce, 29, 30, 35–36, 38

S

Salary expenses, 4–5, 6
Sales taxes, 55
Scheduling of patients, 10, 12–13

Schmitt, Neal, 38
Science Applications International
Corp., 121
Semivariable costs, 82
Situational interviews, 38
Society for Healthcare Strategy and
Market Development, 65
Software
for electronic medical records
systems, 19–25, 99–100
for telephone communications, 12
Solo practice, 78
merging into existing group practice,
79
outside affiliation options for, 82–84
Staff. *See* Employees
Step variable costs, 82
Stephenson, Christy, 86
Structured interviews, 38
Systems analysis. *See* Office systems

T

Tax issues
depreciation, 45
lease/purchase decisions, 42, 45, 55,
56f
real estate taxes, 49
sales taxes, 55
Technology, 98–109
commitment to use of, 108–109
discounts for, 114
E-mail, 105–106
electronic medical records systems,
19–25, 98–105
potential savings from use of,
107–108
purchase decisions for, 108
technical support for, 114
vendors for, 119–121
websites, 14, 107
Telephone systems
automated, 11–12
vs. E-mail, 105
reviewing communications process
for, 11–12